TALENT
IQ

- **IDENTIFY** Your Company's Top Performers
- **IMPROVE** or Remove Underachievers
- **BOOST** Productivity and Profit

Emmett C. Murphy

**PLATINUM
PRESS®**

Published by
Platinum Press®, an imprint of Adams Media,
an F+W Publications Company
57 Littlefield Street, Avon, MA 02322. U.S.A.
www.adamsmedia.com

The Platinum Press® is a registered trademark of F+W Publications, Inc.

ISBN 10: 1-59869-083-3
ISBN 13: 978-1-59869-083-5

Printed in the United States of America

J I H G F E D C B A

Library of Congress Cataloging-in-Publication Data
is available from publisher.

The following terms used in this book are trademarks that are the property
of Emmett C. Murphy: Talent IQ™, LeadershipTalentMapping™, and People
Noise™.

This publication is designed to provide accurate and authoritative information
with regard to the subject matter covered. It is sold with the understanding that
the publisher is not engaged in rendering legal, accounting, or other professional
advice. If legal advice or other expert assistance is required, the services of a
competent professional person should be sought.
—From a *Declaration of Principles* jointly adopted by a Committee of the
American Bar Association and a Committee of Publishers and Associations

Many of the designations used by manufacturers and sellers to distinguish their
product are claimed as trademarks. Where those designations appear in this
book and Adams Media was aware of a trademark claim, the designations have
been printed with initial capital letters.

This book is available at quantity discounts for bulk purchases.
For information, please call 1-800-289-0963.

Dedication

*To Carol
and our parents*

Contents

Acknowledgments

THE TALENTLEADERS OF 983 organizations in virtually every area of business, health care, government, and public service made this book possible. I am immensely grateful for their insights, generosity of spirit, and willingness to put up with my eternal questioning.

While I cannot list them all here, I wish to express thanks to Andy Grove, CEO of Intel; professor Ed Schein and the late Richard Beckhard of MIT; Warren Bruggeman of GE; James Pepicello, M.D., COO and chief medical officer of the Hamot Health Foundation; Don Walsh, VP of IBM; Steve Lampkin, VP of Wal-Mart; Carlos Gutierrez, former CEO of the Kellogg Company (presently Secretary of the U.S. Department of Commerce); Michael Dell, CEO of Dell Computers; Vikesh Mahendroo, past president, William Mercer International; Susan Soong, Taiwan Global Resources; Ingo Hauptman, VP of Hewlett-Packard; Thomas Smith, former CEO of VHA, Inc.; Donna Blancero, Ph.D., Chair, National Society for Hispanic MBA's, Charles Newman, chairman and CEO of the Cambridge Group; Leonard Lopez, chairman and CEO, ESI, Ltd.; D. Wayne Taylor, Ph.D., director, Health Leadership Institute, DeGroote School of Business, McMaster University; Wilson Greatbatch, Ph.D., founder of Wilson Greatbatch, Ltd.; the late professor Gerhard Koch, Ph.D., of the State University of New York; professor James Thrall, M.D., of Harvard Medical School;

Barbara Wolfe, former VP of Lenox Hill Hospital; Christopher Connely, former chair, Healthcare Systems Turnaround Committee; the Archdiocese of New York; and William Shaw, CEO, World Class Shipping.

I am also deeply indebted to my colleagues at EC Murphy Walsh for helping to guide the research and consulting process. Special thanks to my partner, Grant Walsh, whose insights as both a former top-performing CEO and our firm's managing partner were critically important. Sincerest thanks also to Patricia Gorski, a comrade in arms for more than twenty years, and my research associate, Jessica Jochum, for doing some very heavy lifting.

Bringing a manuscript to life is always the greatest challenge. Michael Snell, my mentor, developmental editor, agent, and great friend, shared this journey from the beginning, as he has with all of my books. Without Michael and his lovely wife, Pat, inspiration would have led to perspiration and nothing more.

Michael is one of the greatest TalentLeaders I've ever known and, though he drinks from a perpetual fountain of youth—as reflected in his high-energy, Agassi-like tennis style—he has now coached and developed generations of authors who, like me, are forever in his debt. For them, as well as myself, I say "thank you."

Matching author to publisher and, very important, to editor, is one of Mike's special gifts, which resulted in my partnership with Jill Alexander and the team at Adams Media. Jill and her colleagues were intrigued by the content and committed to the project throughout. Jill's insights into what was most important to the reader were invaluable and reflected her powerful scholarly and practical insight into the complexities of contemporary leadership. Thank you.

Last, and by no means least, I must express my love and appreciation to the chief TalentLeader in my life, my wife, Carol, who still willingly accompanies me on these journeys, and to our parents, Emmett Sr. and Florence, and Tony and Isabelle.

Talent IQ

HE MIGHT HAVE become president of the United States. He certainly possessed the resume of a great American leader: a superb education, dashing good looks, boldness and courage under fire, a remarkable record of achievement at a young age, unwavering dedication to his career, boundless energy, and, most prophetically, unbridled ambition.

After graduating from West Point, he served with distinction throughout the Civil War, becoming the youngest major-general in U.S. military history. The energy he displayed at Bull Run won him a promotion in the Army of the Potomac, and he went on to command the Michigan cavalry brigade at Gettysburg. When the war ended, he accepted a downsized Army's rank of colonel and headed west to the frontier. From there, he expected his fame would spread and culminate in his election to the presidency. Instead, at 4:30 P.M. on June 26, 1876, he led 264 men to their deaths, and his name became synonymous with failure—George Armstrong Custer.

How could so much talent come to such a disastrous end? Who really deserves the blame for Custer's failure? Custer himself, betrayed by his unbridled ambition, or the boss who let that ambition go unchecked?

General Alfred Howe Terry faced a make-or-break decision: choose Lieutenant Colonel George Armstrong Custer to lead the phalanx against the Sioux at the Little Bighorn, or not. While Custer was headstrong, vain, and ambitious beyond measure, he was also talented and had won a reputation as a deadly, brave, and tenacious warrior.

However, serious questions remained. Would Custer follow the carefully crafted plan, or would he abandon it for personal glory? Would he honor the mission? Would he recognize what he didn't know? Would he adapt to the risks at hand or rigidly pursue selfish objectives?

Terry chose unwisely and, as a result, the slaughter of Custer and the Seventh Cavalry at the Little Bighorn remains the most devastatingly complete defeat ever suffered by U.S. military forces. Custer shared the fate of those whose talent, improperly channeled and taken to extremes, sows the seeds of their own downfall.

The failure of talent happens in business every day. Witness the tragedies of Tyco, Enron, and Barclays. Achievement and ambition turn to arrogance; power corrupts; and a sense of invulnerability and infallibility leads to ruin, not only for the talented individual but, even more tragically, for his or her team, organization, and investors as well.

Today, more than ever, an organization's fate depends on its ability to identify, coach, retain, and, when necessary, replace talent. By the same token, talent management determines the success or failure of an individual's career. In a landmark study of CEO success, *Fortune* reported that the failure to surround themselves with talented employees and colleagues was what most accounted for CEO failure and termination, whether measured in terms of profits, shareholder equity, customer loyalty, technological and strategic advantage, or fiduciary integrity.

Regardless of how you measure failure, you know it when you see it: a corporate executive led away in handcuffs, bitter civil and criminal trials, employees robbed of their jobs and pensions, once-mighty corporations mired in bankruptcy.

The reasons are both simple and profound. When leaders fail to surround themselves with talent, when they fail to identify, coach, reward, and retain those who can sustain corporate success, they condemn their organizations to a grim future. Conversely, when they fail to improve or remove those whose behavior puts them and the organization at risk, they commit a form of corporate suicide.

Bad leaders surround themselves with the Custers of the world, and if their own behavior doesn't destroy them, the actions of the Custers will.

The Global Reality

Today, managing talent is every leader's most important job. Successful leaders possess a high Talent IQ. They have become a magnet for talent and the high levels of achievement that great talent invariably produces.

The battle for talent lies at the heart of the worldwide struggle for creative superiority. Technological and scientific innovation is no longer dominated by the West, with the rising numbers of patents and Nobel Prizes from Asia attesting to a dramatic closing of the creative gap. The same applies to what was once thought of as the unassailable U.S. domestic control of business and personal services. Now, multilingual and skilled technicians staff call centers and help desks worldwide, from New Delhi to Rio, providing everything from travel to computer support services.

Early on in this global competition, the American response all too often involved the decimation of talent reserves through indiscriminate downsizing and failure to recognize the dominant role of talent in driving corporate success. Results have since shown that nothing drives productivity more than the preservation and development of talent, and that overzealous and inappropriate cost-cutting undermines an organization's competitiveness.

Other nations, such as China, India, Taiwan, South Korea, and Japan, seem to have grasped these lessons. David Calhoun, CEO of VNU puts it clearly and simply: "There are huge populations out there who are motivated beyond your imagination. That's what you're going to contend with. They didn't grow up with what you had, but they want it and you can't believe how much (they are) trying to get it."

To appreciate the threat, you need only examine the changing global demographics of talent, including declining educational performance in the United States, the rise of outsourcing and offshoring, the aging work force in North America and Europe, and the sudden and drastic decline of achievement among American men. For example, presently, 43 percent of entering freshman in U.S. colleges and universities are men; however, projections indicate that percentage will fall to less than 30 percent within the next decade. Already, the number of U.S. graduates in engineering (95 percent of whom are male) has declined to levels below 30,000, as compared to China, which graduated nearly 500,000 engineers in 2006.

The specific details of many of these changing demographics appear in Appendix B: The Global Demographics of Talent. Smart TalentLeaders would be wise to learn about these trends, as their impact on the global economy will be profound.

Develop Your Talent IQ

Despite all of these factors, the issue of retaining, improving, or replacing talent is ultimately local to an organization and to the people whose hard work and achievement can build and sustain success on a daily and long-term basis.

What concepts and skills—what Talent IQ—do you need to make the most of your own, your team's, and your organization's talent, from the frontlines of customer service to the inner sanctum of the boardroom? How can Talent IQ create a winning advantage for your corporation, employees, shareholders, and, most important, your customers?

This book answers these crucial questions. Based on an extensive ten-year collaborative study (see Appendix C) of best practices among more than 100,000 TalentLeaders in virtually every type of organizational setting, my associates and I at EC Murphy Walsh have uncovered the concepts, skills, and tools anyone can use to boost their Talent IQ. It's not a magic pill you can swallow, but a coherent set of best practices that provides people at every level of an organization with what they need to achieve outstanding performance.

The chapters ahead offer an abundance of real-world examples, concepts, scripts, tools, and assessments that provide a blueprint for developing your Talent IQ. Before reading the chapters, you may wish to pretest your knowledge by taking the Talent IQ Assessment in Appendix A. The questions you'll find there directly relate to this book's chapter-by-chapter content.

The Talent IQ Journey

As my previous book, *Leadership IQ*, emphasized, leadership is not the domain of a privileged few who sit in the CEO's chair. Rather, it is the privilege and responsibility of everyone who works. Every leader works; every worker leads. Hence the word "WorkLeader," which will be used later in this book. We will add another concept to that: Every position requires talent; all talent can be improved. Hence, the word "TalentLeader." As a senior Dell vice president put it, "Leadership flows to the most talented, whether they possess a fiduciary's title or not. The challenge is to identify, develop, and retain the talent we need to guarantee our future. And, here we have to be very accurate and efficient. Competition demands it. It has forced us to evaluate the precision of our thinking and awareness of the risks in not developing and protecting our talent capital." Before we begin the journey toward the optimum use of talent capital, let's take a satellite's-eye view of the trip ahead.

Chapter 1: Build a Culture of Achievement

Our study addressed a most basic question: What is talent? The simplicity of the answer surprised us: *achievement*. Talent that has not yet achieved tangible results is mere potential. All great organizations are driven by the most fundamental of all make-or-break decisions: to build a culture of achievement.

Achievement, we learned, consists of seven distinct principles.

The Seven Principles of Achievement

#1	Embrace Achievement
#2	Be Pragmatic
#3	Practice Strategic Humility
#4	Partner with Your Customer
#5	Make a Total Commitment
#6	Be Optimistic
#7	Accept Responsibility

These principles provide a blueprint for development to build a culture of achievement from the individual on up. Taken together, they stimulate Talent IQ and the ability to achieve more and better results. Such power creates a magnet of hope and leadership influence that overcomes the potential anchor of negativity and failure. With such a magnet in place, TalentLeaders can develop the three pathways through which organizational action takes place on a day-to-day basis: service, innovation, and management.

Chapter 2: Select Achievers

A major breakthrough occurred during our Talent IQ research when we combined the seven principles of achievement with the three pathways through which people accomplish results. It yielded a model we are calling the Achievement in Action Grid. With this grid and its accompanying assessment tools, you can more precisely and comprehensively select the types of behaviors vital to moving your organization forward. We will discuss this grid thoroughly in Chapter 2 and Chapter 4.

Achievement in Action Grid

Paths of Action

The 7 Principles of Achievement		Service	Innovation	Management
	Responsibility	Hero - Achiever	Hero - Achiever	Hero - Achiever
	Optimism	Guide	Discoverer	Problem Solver
	Commitment	Benefactor	Empowerer	Guardian
	Partnership	Empathizer	Knowledge Leader	Builder
	Achievement (pragmatism and humility)	Engager	Seeker	Organizer

As General Terry discovered to his regret, you can easily fall victim to false indicators and pretentious reputations. Successful selection decisions, whether they occur at initial stages of employment or as part of a reselection process, require concrete understanding of personal achievement at all stages of development.

Chapter 3: Coach for Achievement

TalentLeaders are not born; they're coached. Whether it is done through a resident manager or a specially assigned coach or mentor, the most outstanding organizations make the development of talent a one-on-one process.

Over the course of our ten-year research effort we studied the best coaches to determine what, exactly, they did to help people achieve the best results. As we did so, we saw an efficient and coherent coaching process emerge. Tested over three years, a sample of 443 TalentLeaders in executive, middle management, staff, and frontline roles demonstrated an eight-step process that guides them to translate potential into impressive levels of achievement.

The Eight-Step Process

Step 1	Engagement
Step 2	Assessment
Step 3	Diagnosis
Step 4	Planning
Step 5	Execution
Step 6	Evaluation
Step 7	Course Correction
Step 8	Commitment

However, for this process to work, it must remain firmly grounded in the vision and mission of the organization. Too often, we discovered, talent coaching undertaken solely for individual development disconnects people from the realities of the organization and its unique goals. Coaching should help galvanize an individual to pursue those goals relentlessly.

Chapter 4: Improve or Remove Talent-on-the-Bubble

While talent intent on achievement can transform an organization for the better, talent run amok can create chaos—an anchor of negativity and irresponsibility. Therefore, you must not only harness the behaviors that produce achievement; you must also deal with the behaviors that can destroy an organization. These behaviors define a condition we call "talent-on-the-bubble." Those in this state can compromise the achievement of others and create a cycle of irresponsibility that requires another make-or-break decision—to improve or remove.

Recognizing and dealing with talent-on-the-bubble is crucial, because talent-on-the-bubble behavior can metastasize like a cancer. As with cancer, you must treat it on several levels simultaneously. The first level involves refocusing and retraining behavior. Here coaching, evaluation, and reinforcement come into play. This represents noninvasive therapies. However, when surgery is required, you must perform it with a sharp scalpel.

A specific study of 110 TalentLeaders who were on-the-bubble produced two significant findings. First, coaching *does* work. And second, a relatively small but dangerous percentage (20 percent to 30 percent) won't respond to even the best coaching. The chapter will offer proven scripts for dealing with this challenge.

Talent-on-the-Bubble Grid

	Service	Innovation	Management
Fence-Sitting	Procrastinator	Narcissist	Stonewaller
Avoidance	Martyr	Deer in Headlights	Curmudgeon
Hostility	Gossip and Critic	Black Hole	Bully
Contempt	Manipulator	Fetalist	Bomber
Irresponsibility	Backstabber	Suicide	Predator

Chapter 5: Communicate Commitment

Because you must maintain connection to the people who count the most, you must become a master communicator. Bill Shaw, CEO of World Class Shipping, explains it this way: "Our service partners are spread all over the globe. They are our most important asset and they need to know they're never alone, that we will always be there for them, no matter what personal, operational, or customer challenge they face. But, this takes more than wanting to do the right thing. It takes a total commitment to communicating that commitment by cutting through the interference, chaos, and cross-talk—the noise—that can undermine timely and clear communication."

Bill and his team have adopted a new way of diagnosing communication chaos that helps them get their message out every day to a worldwide network. Like other TalentLeaders, they've learned how to diagnose and quiet noise, including interference, attenuation, resistance, cross-talk, and glitches. This chapter shares this innovation and the practical steps you can take to implement it in your own organization.

Chapter 6: Measure Responsibility

From the individual to the partner, team, and organization as a whole, achievement must remain the focus of evaluation, measurement, and subsequent reward. Without such continuity and cohesiveness, no one can reliably develop an achievement culture, let alone one that maximizes talent. Too often, evaluation on the individual level does not match evaluation at department, service-line, and organizational levels.

Our research underscores the saying that "what you measure is what you stand for." Any inconsistency will blur goals, objectives, and the overall mission throughout the organization and end up fueling negativity. Thus, great organizations utilize consistent achievement and mission-focused measurement criteria up and down the organizational ladder. Taken together, these criteria create a cultural achievement assessment that reliably establishes a unified cultural context while providing a practical method for teams, departments, and individuals to assess their performance in relation to specific mission goals and objectives.

Chapter 7: Improve Team IQ

Successful teams are not born; they are developed. Like successful individuals, teams require expert coaching that employs a specific achievement protocol emphasizing intelligence, problem-solving, and a commitment to mission.

Our investigation unveiled an extraordinarily varied and confusing array of team-building techniques. Few focused on problem-solving and the mobilization of talent for achievement. Instead, most addressed internal social priorities of protocol, relationship development, and power sharing. Without a focus on the larger issues of vision and mission achievement, such team processes usually floundered.

To address these problems, we isolated, documented, refined, and tested processes for the development of team intelligence and problem-solving acumen, or "Team IQ." The resulting assessment-driven problem-solving process emphasizes the need for measurable results, including cost-effectiveness. As teams received systematic coaching in this new problem-solving process, they racked up measurably higher accomplishments.

Fortunately, the same process applies to both executive and nonmanagement teams. The content may vary, but the core process does not.

Chapter 8: Manage Conflict—Now!

How do you get superstar achievement? When we compared the top 5 percent of TalentLeaders with all other TalentLeaders, we isolated another make-or-break decision: the decision to manage conflict swiftly and decisively!

Talented people can produce outstanding results, but they can also cause and suffer intense conflict. More than 90 percent of TalentLeaders believed that their superiors did not successfully address the issues surrounding stress and conflict. This finding prompted us to devise better techniques for resolving conflict. Since old-style management strategies often prove too cumbersome and imprecise to resolve most conflicts, we have translated the practices of the most outstanding leaders into a clear set of guidelines for conflict resolution.

Chapter 9: Design a Leadership Talent Map for the Future

How do we put the right people in the right place for now *and* the future? Every organization wrestles with this fundamental question. Yet, if leaders don't draw a map of how their talented people do what they do, and whether they are, in fact, in the right place at the right time to do it effectively and productively, they can neither align their talent for present needs nor accurately plan for succession and the challenges in the future.

All too often, when leaders attempt to address this issue, they rely on traditional succession planning or productivity analysis. However, as the Talent IQ research revealed, doing so alienates more than 90 percent of the very people that the leaders need in order to address both immediate and future needs. In response to this reality, we developed Talent Imaging™. As Dennis Chow, CEO of a major electronics distributor, put it, "Of all the challenges we face, making sure we have the right people in the right place . . . worries us most. Not only do our people change, but so do our needs.

"However, since we've begun Talent Imaging in earnest, we've been able to turn what was an ever-present fear into a continuously flowing process of team collaboration and visioning for the future. A very important key was changing our thinking from 'succession,' which made people think they were dispensable—perhaps immediately—to 'progression,' which included everyone in moving forward toward new opportunities."

Chapter 9 explains how Talent Imaging works, and provides a simple five-part mapping protocol.

Conclusion: The Talent Imperative

Stunning performance. World-class achievement. Spectacular results. All of these are hard to attain, harder yet to maintain, and even harder to surpass. Our research reinforced something we always knew: that for people and organizations to become great and remain great and become even greater, they must make talent their imperative and create a plan to translate it into everyday action.

Getting Started

Let's set to work boosting your Talent IQ. Before you proceed to Chapter 1, however, you may want to pause and take the Talent IQ Assessment in Appendix A. That will give you a benchmark to which you can refer as you move through the book. In the end you may look back and see that you've come a long way toward joining the ranks of world-class TalentLeaders.

CHAPTER 1

Build a Culture of Achievement

DURING THE POST–World War II boom in higher education, with hundreds of thousands of servicemen taking advantage of the GI Bill, college textbook publishing was a growth industry, one that required talented people in every job. James F. Leisy, the founder and CEO of Wadsworth, one of the most successful and innovative startups of the time, knew that talent, more than any other factor, would make or break his fledgling enterprise. As a result of his ability to build a corporate culture of achievement, Wadsworth grew in a few short years to become a major player in its field.

Unlike many CEOs, Jim Leisy worked in the trenches of talent-building every day. Since acquisitions editors—the people who created new product—rose from the sales force, Jim would personally interview promising recruits. "He made you feel as if the company's whole future depended on you," recalls one former executive who flourished under Leisy's mentorship. "His annual editorial retreats didn't just teach and motivate us. They instilled in us the esprit de corps of an elite Marine commando unit."

A lucrative profit-sharing program kept all eyes focused on productivity and profitability. When, however, talented editors, yearning for more power and independence, grew restless and were at risk of straying off to join the competition at an executive level, Jim would reward and challenge them with a startup company of

1

their own under the Wadsworth umbrella. That retention strategy spawned such successful publishers as Wadsworth's Brooks/Cole and Duxbury subsidiaries. Loyalty ran so deep at Wadsworth that not one key editor left during the 1960s and 1970s, with the exception of a few talented people who just could not improve their poor performance, despite intensive coaching by Leisy and his managers.

According to Thomas Martin, a Wadsworth author and the retired president of the Illinois Institute of Technology, "[Leisy] was phenomenally successful as a catalyst. He strongly embraced what was known then and now as 'the HP way' [the Hewlett-Packard way]—management-by-walking-around, close relationships with all employees, and assembling highly motivated people who felt personal ownership in what they were doing. Higher education publishing is a very entrepreneurial business and the Wadsworth culture fostered by Leisy encouraged that."

Creativity. Achievement. Loyalty. Productivity. Profitability. These results came about because Jim Leisy and his managers used their Talent IQ to create a culture of achievement.

Why build a culture of achievement? Because it performs better than one whose people define themselves, and the work, through affiliation and power. The former know that success depends on *what you know and what you can do.* The latter care more about *who you know and what power you wield.*

When, during our Talent IQ research, we compared the achievement-driven organizations with those dominated by a sense of affiliation and power, we found extraordinary differences.

Achievement-driven organizations:

- Were 250 percent more profitable.
- Experienced markedly higher rates of "customer willingness to return."
- Offered incentive-based compensation to four times as many employees as did low-performing organizations.

Affiliative and power-driven organizations:

- Lost $300 billion in 2000 due to disengaged and irresponsible employees.
- Suffered from the disillusionment of managers and executives.

In addition, within those organizations:

- 76 percent of senior executives thought that their frontline and middle managers resisted responsibility for performance.
- 91 percent of CEOs thought that their frontline and middle managers resisted responsibility.
- 78 percent of senior executives felt that their managers lacked sufficient skill to manage underachievers.
- 90 percent of frontline managers believed they needed improvement in managing underachievement.

The results shown above underscore the significant advantages of achievement-driven organizations. The question is, how do you build such a culture?

To find the answer, we conducted an extensive Cultural Survey that measured culture-building practices in more than 1,100 organizations representing a wide range of industries, from health care to high technology. As we analyzed the results, three dominant points emerged. Achievement-driven cultures:

1. Observe seven principles that guide the identification, selection, coaching, rewarding, retention, retraining, and replacement of talent from the frontlines to the boardroom.
2. Leverage achievement to create a Magnet of Influence. In other words, place those who achieve in leadership positions at all levels of your organization and emphasize their role in driving corporate progress.
3. Develop the three paths to achievement in the workplace: service, innovation, management.

The Seven Principles of Achievement

What is talent? The TalentLeaders in our study offered a simple and direct answer: achievement. Talent that has not achieved concrete and tangible results represents mere potential, a "maybe" at best and a deceit at worst, an unknown that is as yet unworthy of the trust required to move individuals, organizations, and societies from one level to the next.

Definition of Work

Physicists define *work* as pushing or pulling something through a distance. If you stand at the base of the Empire State Building and push until you collapse from exhaustion but have not budged the skyscraper an inch, you have not done any work!

Measurable achievement consists of a continuum of seven behavioral principles that TalentLeaders both preach and practice in their work and personal lives. These guiding principles (which we first mentioned in the Introduction) provide a blueprint for development that talent coaches can incorporate into daily operational management, as well as use for assessment of individual, team, and organizational strengths. Each of the principles includes a specific cluster of behaviors and traits that anyone can use for establishing performance criteria and measuring progress throughout an organization, from the boiler room to the boardroom.

The Seven Principles of Achievement

#1	Embrace Achievement
#2	Be Pragmatic
#3	Practice Strategic Humility
#4	Partner with Your Customer
#5	Make a Total Commitment
#6	Be Optimistic
#7	Accept Responsibility

Principle 1: Embrace Achievement

Achievement means . . .

- Advancing through your own accomplishments.
- Seeking recognition for success based on your own efforts.
- Attaining realistic but challenging goals to get ahead.

Andy Grove, former chairman and CEO of Intel Corporation, has often been recognized as an achiever. However, such recognition emerged from humble beginnings. Born in Hungary, Grove and his family fled the tyranny of Soviet oppression for the promise of the United States, arriving in New York City penniless, yet motivated to begin their new life.

While moving to a new country that has an entirely different culture and language would overwhelm many people, it barely fazed Andy Grove, who immediately immersed himself in the new life his parents had given him. Through diligence and perseverance, Grove overcame the language barrier and worked his way through the City University of New York and, eventually, the University of California at Berkeley, where he received a PhD in physics. Success came easily in business, as well, as Grove became a world-class industry and technology leader, and one of the designers of a revolutionary computer chip. No one could deny that Andy Grove had put his talent to excellent use. He was highly successful by anyone's measure.

But, in the fall of 1994, something went very wrong for him. At age 58, he learned that he had prostate cancer. After a series of tests, Grove's urologist phoned him at the office with news that would alter Andy Grove's life forever: "Andy, you have a tumor. It's mainly on the right side; there's a tiny bit on the left. It's a moderately aggressive one."

At first, Grove went into denial about the diagnosis of the life-threatening illness. He assumed a passive position, consigning responsibility for managing this drastic change in his life to the "experts."

Soon, however, he became restless and disappointed in himself for not applying the life lessons he had learned as an immigrant, a business leader, and a scientist. He decided to reassert the achievement ethic he had practiced throughout his career and take control of the situation himself.

As Grove reasserted control, he developed a new daily routine that included in-depth searches in medical databases, online resources, and medical magazines for any and all information about prostate cancer. He applied his talent as a superb researcher to a new topic, tracking down articles and research reports that he passed on to the experts who were overseeing his care. Nightly, Grove's wife trekked to the library for copies of the articles that her husband had catalogued during the day. Grove got second opinions, third opinions, and real-life accounts from others who had overcome prostate cancer.

Ultimately, he combined all his research, his own test results, information from ongoing conversations with prostate cancer patients, oncologists, surgeons, and other doctors, and created a chart of all the possible treatment options, their side effects, and the probabilities of recurrence. Just as he had organized resources to address other challenges in his life, he applied his analytical talent to help him decide how to tackle his disease and achieve a good result.

Andy Grove eventually settled upon a new, but promising, treatment option that involved implanting near the tumor eight pinlike tubes, through which doctors would insert radioactive "seeds" for a short period of time. After receiving this focused high-dose radiation treatment, Grove underwent twenty-eight daily doses of external radiation, which took no more than a few minutes each. He would walk to a local hospital at 7:30 in the morning and then arrive at work for a full day by 8:30.

Six months after the start of treatment, Andy Grove reclaimed his life—100 percent cancer-free. By refusing to allow external forces to control his fate, Grove embraced achievement.

Consistently, across every organization we studied, TalentLeaders share the belief that how you choose to move forward in life makes all the difference between success and failure. TalentLeaders have learned that self-reliance and personal competence precede self-respect and success, that success depends on personal achievement in the frontlines of work, that *what you know and can do* matters more than who you know and what power you wield. Achievement always trumps affiliation and power. Accomplishment always trumps manipulation and control.

The social scientist David McClelland noted that civilizations—and businesses—rise and fall based on the belief structures of their people. For those driven by the need for affiliation, advancement devolves into manipulation. Cultures in which control rules the day inevitably decline as the value of achievement gives way to privilege, and rewards for service to the many—citizens and customers—give way to rewards for service to the few.

Similarly, for those people in which a drive for power dominates, advancement becomes a control game. Cultures in which control rules the day also inevitably decline, as the struggle to dominate or be dominated destroys the bonds of trust that lead to a mutual commitment to service and progress.

By contrast, achievement-driven cultures define advancement as a consequence of reaching goals, attaining objectives, and getting results. Such cultures grow and prosper as accomplishment leads to progress, and as rewards for merit encourage people to serve, innovate, and organize to improve the common good.

Principle 2: Be Pragmatic

When it came to selecting engineers, Thomas Edison was extremely pragmatic. He'd give the applicant a light bulb and ask, "How much water will it hold?" Most candidates would calculate the bulb's volume mathematically, an approach that takes twenty minutes or more. The smart ones, however, would fill the bulb with water and then pour its contents into a measuring cup, a procedure that takes less than one minute. Which engineer do you think Edison hired?

Like Edison, the TalentLeaders in our study are pragmatists. In a world of constant and even accelerating change, they know that adopting and taking advantage of change requires an unflagging ability to question and probe for solutions to problems. The pragmatist understands that abstract ideas have value to the extent that they can be translated into a solution for a tangible problem. Idealism paves the path to stagnation and business death. Problem-solving is as practical as tying your shoes or filling the bulb with water. Mere thought alone will never get the job done.

Pragmatism means . . .

- Searching for the facts yourself and concentrating on the most workable solution.
- Believing form must follow function.
- Preferring simple solutions to complex strategies.
- Making decisions after objectively assessing a situation and identifying a well-reasoned course of action.

TalentLeaders are scientists at heart, approaching each situation with an understanding that facts must govern action, that what works matters more than what looks good, that the simplest solution in always the best solution. That's why TalentLeaders love questioning and probing. They remain responsible skeptics, always asking "Why is this important?" and "How can we do it better?"

Principle 3: Practice Strategic Humility

"I DON'T WANT TO MAKE THE WRONG MISTAKE."—YOGI BERRA

When competent, strong-willed people recognize that they lack the knowledge to solve a problem, they do something about it. They don't cover up their ignorance. They practice strategic humility. That is, when you know where you want to go (strategy), admit that you don't know exactly how to get there (humility), and ask for help, you're practicing strategic humility. Admitting a lack of knowledge or expertise, and seeking help to acquire it, requires self-confidence. Of course, self-confidence doesn't come easily when we feel inadequate. It always pays off, however, as the meteoric success of Ben & Jerry's ice cream company proves.

Ben Cohen and Jerry Greenfield first met in seventh-grade gym class. They quickly became close friends because, as they put it, they shared a "deep and sincere appreciation of good food and lots of it." After high school, they initially went their separate ways but always maintained a close friendship. While Ben drove an ice cream truck for $100 a week and all the ice cream he could eat, Jerry enrolled in college to prepare for medical school.

When Jerry graduated from college and couldn't get into medical school, the two friends put their heads together and thought about their futures. "We just wanted to do something that would be fun," Ben explains in their cookbook, *Ben & Jerry's Double Dip*, whose introduction describes the history of their business. "We wanted to be our own bosses and work exactly when, where, and how we wanted." True to their original interests, they came up with the idea to open a little restaurant and feature one of their favorite foods, ice cream. Next, they picked their dream location: rural Vermont.

When Ben and Jerry started their business in 1978, they expected the venture to last a few years, until they found something else to do. They certainly didn't expect runaway success that made their names synonymous with gourmet ice cream. From the outset the partners built their business around the concept of "linked prosperity," which ensured that all employees shared in the profits of the corporation. This was part of a strategic vision for success based on broad-based collaboration, sharing, and recognition that sustained success would require delegation and a concrete sense of shared ownership.

Then, in 1995, after nearly two decades of success, Ben Cohen and Jerry Greenfield found themselves in a difficult situation. The

9

demand for their product was greater than their ability to satisfy it. When it became clear that they lacked the knowledge to take the business to the next level, they practiced strategic humility yet again and began searching for a compatible chief executive officer to take over the reins. Of course, they sought someone who would, unlike many bottom-line-obsessed CEOs, embrace the idea of "linked prosperity."

After an extensive search, they chose Robert Holland Jr. for the job. It was a smart choice. The new CEO successfully steered the company through its big growth stage without losing touch with the leaders' principled business practices.

Ben and Jerry knew where they wanted their company to go, but admitted that they lacked certain knowledge to take it there, and sought help. In short, they practiced strategic humility. And it paid off.

Humility means . . .

- Understanding that you have a lot to learn.
- Admitting mistakes, then learning from them.
- Believing you "can't do it alone," that sometimes you need to rely on others.
- Asking questions when discussing issues with others to ensure you understand all relevant points of view, especially ones with which you initially disagree.

TalentLeaders are perpetual students. Though they exude self-confidence and possess healthy egos, they never pass up an opportunity to learn. Wishing not to make the "wrong" mistake, they search high and low for new facts and more accurate information. That's why the term *strategic* humility is used in this book. While not noted for extreme modesty, TalentLeaders nevertheless realize the strategic weakness of arrogance and the unwillingness to admit it.

Our research reminded me of experiences I had early in my career with Lee Iacocca, the former chairman and CEO of Chrysler.

Known to the general public as a charming and confident spokes-man, always ready with an answer and opinion, those of us who worked with him in addressing strategic and operational problems saw him as an incredibly tenacious questioner, always challenging and probing for weaknesses, threats, alternatives, and solutions. In an industry known for the thick-headedness of its leaders, he dem-onstrated intellectual curiosity and flexibility, defining his role as a student in search of the best solution. His usual script for meet-ings was to begin with a reiteration of the immediate objective at hand followed by rigorous questioning of what each of us had learned about achieving it. I remember vividly the first time I was on the receiving end of those questions. I learned quickly that being a student of and with Iacocca meant intensive preparation and a willingness to rethink the obvious.

Principle 4: Partner with Your Customer

Partnership means . . .

- Believing you are a partner to your customers.
- Understanding that working with others is a chance to col-laborate in achievement.
- Finding a solution that results in mutual understanding when a disagreement arises.

We are born to serve. Our humanity requires it. Not everyone serves for the same reason, however. Some feel a sense of obliga-tion, or reciprocity. Others may do so less willingly in the bonds of servitude. Philip Diehl, former director of the U.S. Mint, served for the right reasons.

When Diehl started at the Mint in 1994, the agency looked like a holdover from the Industrial Revolution, and a poorly man-aged one at that. At that time the Mint turned out 20 billion coins per year, and it monitored all the coins in circulation, all without an automated tracking system. That made it impossible to match production to demand.

Even more antiquated was the customer service center that took mail orders for collectibles and commemoratives. Employees, crowded together in cramped rooms in a converted warehouse shared with the U.S. Postal Service, lost valuable time several times a day when the discovery of a suspicious package forced evacuation of the building. This Dickensian environment produced terrible customer service, with the average order taking more than eight weeks to fill. As Diehl recalls, "There was no sense of urgency about the problem, or even awareness that there was a problem."

Amazingly, the Mint had gotten so disconnected from its customers that standard policy forbade employees from ever communicating with them. In addition, prior to 1992, the Office of Management and Budget (OMB) discouraged agencies from spending money on some of the more common customer service tools available to businesses—market research, focus groups, and customer satisfaction surveys. If someone managed to untangle a snarl and launch a customer survey, that task required a six-month OMB approval process. Frustrated with this monumental obstacle, Diehl decided to contact his customers personally.

Diehl "went undercover" as a coin collector at coin conventions around the country, chatting with fellow collectors about their needs. Through his personal "focus group" research, Diehl discovered the cause of the Mint's declining revenues and prestige. The "eight weeks to infinity" delivery process for coin orders, coupled with the Mint's strict prepayment policy, meant that customers consigned their money to limbo waiting for a product that might never arrive. Explains Diehl, "Most people at the Mint, and especially the people in customer service, believed their job was to protect the assets of the U.S. government. . . . Before we send you your coins, we're going to make sure that your check clears. . . . We really believed that customers were trying to defraud the government. Today, we have gone to the other extreme—the customer is king."

With a new vision in place, Diehl convened a task force that established performance goals more suited to private industry than a government agency. Although modest at first, these initiatives touched off a wave of improvements at the Mint, including a migration to the Web for order processing. After implementing its customer service goals, the Mint gained permission to participate in the American Customer Satisfaction Index and found itself ranked second in the United States, just after Mercedes-Benz North America.

However, Diehl was not satisfied with merely improving efficiency. He and his team began to rethink not only how they did business, but also the nature of the agency itself, eventually concluding that the Mint was not just in the money business, but in the education and relationship business. At root, coin collecting is a hobby: a way for generations of family and friends to forge stronger relationships while learning about history. As Diehl discovered, "Coin collectors have always known that coins have two functions in society. Primarily, coins facilitate commerce. But also important, coinage has always been used to tell the story of our nation and its own people." Marketing Director David Pickens, reflecting on the previously stodgy nature of the federal agency, adds, "We had forgotten the magic of our product."

To recapture the magic, the Mint launched its most successful initiative to date—the 50 State Quarters Program, which, like most changes at the Mint, came at the behest of customers. The results, Diehl points out, have been phenomenal. "How many companies have introduced a product that will sell more than 4 billion units in its first year and be touched by every person in the country?"

Philip Diehl clearly demonstrates the importance of making partnership everyone's job. As a civil servant nearing retirement, he could have let the Mint cruise along in the breakdown lane. Instead, he personally chose to circumvent the barriers to customer partnership and build durable relationships with his organization's customers.

13

The TalentLeaders we studied consistently demonstrated an intense commitment to partnership, with other individuals, with their team and organization, and, most important, with all the organization's stakeholders, especially its customers. Talented people extend their belief in their own ability to others, valuing the importance of everyone who benefits from their talent. They identify with customers' needs because they understand that they share those needs themselves.

This reality emerged quite clearly during a special study we conducted to compare a sample of TalentLeaders with mediocre performers in a wide variety of positions in many different organizations. Mediocre performers often saw themselves as functionaries, bureaucrats, and bystanders in their relationship to customers, while TalentLeaders saw themselves as partners. When asked to draw a picture of their relationship, TalentLeaders came up with this:

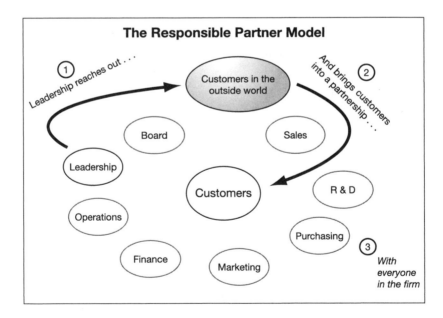

TalentLeaders placed customers in the center of the organizational structure, rather than on the outside. It reflects a true customer focus that views the customer not as an outsider but as a strategic partner. When asked to describe their concept of "partner," TalentLeaders noted the power of reciprocity and their belief that what you generously give you receive back in abundance. They accept responsibility to serve as guardian of the customer's interests and as advocate for the customer with internal constituencies that may not fully grasp the power and importance of the partnership. In such a partnership, the customers repaid the service they received with loyalty and trust.

Principle 5: Make a Total Commitment

"PLEASE DON'T TELL ME ABOUT COMMITMENT. I KNOW WHAT IT MEANS."
—KATHERINE LOPEZ, ONCOLOGY NURSE

I recently received a major dose of "humility" during evening rounds at a prominent academic medical center where I was serving as interim CEO during a difficult turnaround. At the time I was sharing the early findings of our Talent IQ research with medical and nursing staff, particularly focusing on the power of commitment in the clinical setting. During rounds that night, an oncology nurse approached me. "Please don't tell me about commitment," she said. "I know what it means. It means staying with my patients to the end, whether that means they get to go home or not."

We all make commitments every day—to coworkers, spouses, children, friends, and relations. But how many of us make a "life or death" commitment each and every day?

For a clinical oncology nurse, the "or not" is a true test of commitment. The ability to make a total commitment marks a momentous turning point for talented people. It often requires maturity, not just in years, but in a sense of what really matters in life. Stress research has demonstrated the value of staying the course and following through on difficult challenges, a trait that frequently develops as people mature to higher levels of personal development and fulfillment.

Commitment means . . .

- Believing it's important to follow through on work you've started.
- Accepting the fact that you can't learn what you need to know if you don't follow through.
- Focusing on long-term success.
- Being personally "present" to empower and energize others.
- Displaying patience, persistence, and professionalism in the face of obstacles and setbacks.

As talented people move along the continuum from achievement to pragmatism, strategic humility, and partnership, they naturally develop a more complete picture of their humanity and that of others. This increased understanding unleashes, in turn, higher levels of contribution. Partnership triggers a realization of both the profound benefits of following through and the disastrous costs of quitting. Commitment is the glue that holds it all together. *Commitment is not just abstract philosophy; it's a concrete protocol of behavior.* Once you make contact—with a colleague, a superior, a new recruit, or a customer—you can either climb the commitment ladder to success or sink into a swamp of negativity and failure.

In our relationships, we make choices regarding commitment every time we make contact. When we choose awareness and involvement, we develop empathy and the capacity to understand others' needs and aspirations. Such empathy propels the desire to empower and share information that can make a positive difference in another's life. And, as we empower, we resolve to sustain our relationship as we move toward achievement. This behavior supports partnership and sets the stage for hope and responsibility.

When talent-on-the-bubble chooses avoidance and indifference, fear and hostility build until they culminate in contempt, a sure sign of impending failure.

For TalentLeaders, commitment translates ambition into action and action into results. TalentLeaders demonstrate patience, persistence, and professionalism, following through to achievement.

Principle 6: Be Optimistic

Optimism means . . .

- Believing there's a solution to every problem.
- Eliminating negative attributes and beliefs.
- Learning to cope with adversity and succeed despite the odds.
- Viewing setbacks as opportunities to learn and achieve.

Franklin Delano Roosevelt was one of the most confident and, some might say, arrogant leaders in American history. He waded readily into any dilemma with the air of someone who believed he could solve a problem by the sheer force of his will, intellect, and charm. But behind this public image, the real Roosevelt was a man who, due to his battle with polio, had developed a deep humility, a keen awareness of his need for others, and the firm resolve to live that only profound optimism can make possible. While his illness left him physically battered, the battle to overcome it had taught him the true meaning of achievement, and the way in which partnership and commitment fuel optimism and creative solutions.

Because his ability to move was so severely restricted, Roosevelt surrounded himself with what he called "personal listeners," people in key posts who could go out into the world and collect the information he needed to make the decisions that a world leader must make. He used these listeners as virtual physical extensions of himself—his eyes and ears and legs.

One of Roosevelt's key listeners was a childhood friend, Livingston W. Houston, who later became president of the Rensselaer Polytechnic Institute in Troy, New York, and who was a world-renowned scientist and humanitarian in his own right. During the period just preceding the Second World War, FDR asked Houston to serve as his "personal listener" and as an undersecretary in the Department of the Navy. A close personal friend of FDR's from the president's college and early polio years, Houston, like FDR, believed that the only thing they had to fear was fear itself.

One day Houston was lunching with a naval captain who appeared deeply distressed. "What's wrong?" Houston asked him. The captain, with an air of despondence, outlined his grave concerns over the ability of America's warships to protect themselves in the event of an air attack. The navy's policies were outdated, he said, but he could not get any of the navy brass to listen to his concerns.

When Houston pressed for details, the captain described the several different stations on board each battleship and the rules, or "gunnery command policies," that governed how these stations would respond to an attack. These policies stated that each individual station on board each ship should choose its own targets.

"I don't see a problem with that strategy," Houston responded.

The navy captain forged on. "These policies were set over 100 years ago! Today, a single airplane can carry enough ammunition to inflict fatal damage to one of our warships, and these planes can reach speeds of up to 400 miles per hour in a dive! What if only *one* of the gunnery commanders on board a ship chooses to target an aircraft diving in at that speed because the others have independently decided to focus on floating targets, or more distant craft?"

Houston asked one last question: "How do you propose to solve the problem, then?" The captain, relieved, and more than a little surprised that the undersecretary showed such an interest in his concerns, told Houston that the solution lay in synchronizing all the gunnery posts under one command in the event of attack. In that way, firepower could be concentrated in sufficient force to give the ship a reasonable chance of destroying a plane zooming in from an almost vertical angle. In the event of an attack by more than one plane, firepower could be divided as equally as possible to concentrate on both incoming craft. This would require a central gunnery command, a major change in battleship protocol.

Houston wondered aloud why the captain had not explained this problem to the navy's admirals and the secretary of war. To this, the captain responded, "Well, I've tried. I've tried for over six months to convince them! They say it flies in the face of tradition, and that if I don't shut up, I will be cashiered out of the navy."

The undersecretary knew what to do—sidestep the navy brass and take the matter directly to their boss: the commander in chief. Would the captain meet with the president of the United States and air his concerns? In a heartbeat.

At 5:30 the next morning, the captain presented the facts to the president at a brief pre-dawn meeting. During the next thirty days, whenever the president met with his military advisers, he inserted into his discussions the question of gunnery command in the event of an aerial attack. The constant pressure initiated a spiral of activity that led to a review of the naval captain's proposal and a permanent change in naval tactical policies, which saved countless American lives from kamikaze attacks during World War II.

Achievement, like happiness, is never guaranteed, but you have the right to pursue it. Only pessimism can stop you. Studies of battlefield commanders have revealed the power of optimism when making life-and-death decisions. Commanders who framed decisions in terms of possibility instead of loss suffered less than half the casualty rate of other commanders, and enjoyed more than three times the likelihood of victory. Studies confirmed that the brain-wave patterns of excellent commanders indicated higher levels of creativity and breakthrough insights.

Not only does optimism increase the likelihood of attaining happiness, it increases the possibility of achievement, partnership, commitment and, most important, responsibility.

Principle 7: Accept Responsibility

Responsibility means . . .

- Accepting the consequences of your decisions and actions, whether positive or negative.
- Working to correct any negative consequences of your decisions or actions.
- Accepting that others are not to blame for your mistakes.

When Aaron Feuerstein's company, the Malden Mills, burned to the ground a few years ago, his actions demonstrated the true meaning of "accept responsibility." The Malden Mills textile factory in Methuen, Massachusetts, was established by Feuerstein's grandfather in 1907. Aaron Feuerstein has lived in New England all of his life and, when he inherited the business, he maintained his loyalty to his community, keeping the company in Massachusetts while his competitors abandoned the United States for countries where they could pay employees only a few cents an hour. He knew that the town of Methuen would turn into a ghost town if he pulled out, taking with him the 2,400 jobs supplied by the Mills.

This sense of responsibility did not come cheap, and Malden Mills suffered serious financial troubles during the early 1980s. Even when the company declared bankruptcy, however, Feuerstein did not give up. Rather, he set about finding a company-saving idea, a product that would revive Malden Mills' flagging fortunes. His research and development team, which he kept working throughout the financial crisis, did not disappoint him. In the nick of time, they announced that they had developed a lightweight, warm, quick-to-dry, and easy-to-dye fabric made mostly of recycled plastic. It was the perfect product to compete in the fake fur market, which had cut into the demand for the synthetic fabrics from Malden Mills. The environmentally responsible, lightweight fabric—named "Polartec"—appealed both to consumers and to clothing manufacturers, especially those who made winter sports apparel.

Almost overnight such companies as L.L. Bean, Eastern Mountain Sports, Lands' End, Patagonia, and Eddie Bauer were featuring the fabric in their outerwear products. By 1995, Polartec sales had doubled the revenue for Malden Mills, accounting for half of its $400-million-plus income that year.

It looked like smooth sailing for the company at that point. The townspeople of Methuen felt more secure than ever before, as did Aaron Feuerstein himself. Then everything went terribly wrong, when one night during the winter of 1995, a boiler at the factory exploded, causing a raging fire that injured twenty-seven employees and leveled three of the manufacturer's buildings. An employee at the Mills described the catastrophe: "I was standing there seeing the mill burn with my son, who also works there, and he looked at me and said, 'Dad, I think we just lost our jobs.' Years of our lives seemed gone."

In fact, the livelihood of the entire city seemed doomed. The seventy-year-old Feuerstein would, many assumed, just collect his insurance money and retire. Or, perhaps he would use this turn of events as an excuse to relocate the business overseas.

Three days after the fire, Feuerstein gathered more than 1,000 people at a local high school gym and announced, "For the next thirty days—and it might be more—all our employees will be paid their full salaries. By January second, we will be fully operational." The gym erupted in cheers and hugs.

The company's customers, including L.L. Bean, pledged their support. Within days, $330,000 arrived from various companies, the Bank of Boston, the needletrades union, and a local chamber of commerce. Letters of support, some with modest donations, came from all over the country.

Feuerstein's initial time-frame estimates proved overly optimistic. Ninety days came and went, then another ninety, and another. Rebuilding would take much more time and money than he had anticipated. However, this did not weaken Aaron Feuerstein's resolve. True to his word, he kept rebuilding until, in September 1997, the company held its grand reopening, almost two years after the explosion. Incredibly, the Mills rehired 97.4 percent of the workers who had lost their jobs due to the fire. At the opening, Feuerstein expressed his intention of calling the last seventy employees back to work soon. He would not rest easy until he had reunited the entire Malden Mills family.

Responsibility, coupled with optimism, can achieve miracles. When TalentLeaders choose to accept responsibility, they initiate ever more powerful cycles of learning and accomplishment. That choice binds together all seven principles of achievement, uniting them into a durable lever that can move mountains.

Leverage the Power of Achievement

In any group, whether in a classroom, in an office, or on a battlefield, each individual possesses a measure of talent, but not everyone achieves the A-level accomplishment of a Jim Leisy, an Andy Grove, or an Aaron Feuerstein. The group usually represents a bell-shaped curve, with poor performers at one end, many talent-on-the-bubble performers in the middle, and superstars at the other end.

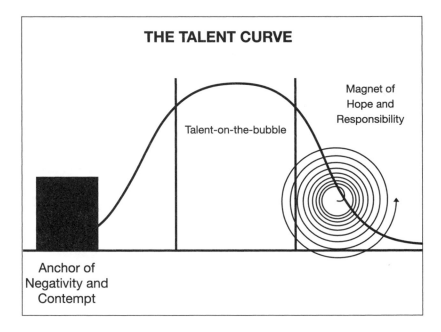

THE TALENT CURVE

Talent-on-the-bubble

Magnet of
Hope and
Responsibility

Anchor of
Negativity and
Contempt

In a culture of achievement, the most outstanding performers serve as models and inspiration for the majority who need improvement. They create a magnet of achievement, partnership, and responsibility that can attract everyone in the organization toward success. Only then can careful coaching move talented people "off-the-bubble." We'll explore coaching later, but now we need to grasp that the talent curve addresses the critical question, "What can I do to move myself, my team, and my organization to a higher level of achievement?" Those who can move to this higher level of achievement should be retained; those who can't should be replaced.

On a practical level, this raises a reality of leadership that is rarely addressed: political power. All leadership involves the leveraging of power. As we will discuss in Chapter 2, "affiliators" look at power as a matter of manipulation, and controllers as a function of coercion.

Too often, achievement leaders mistakenly believe that their personal achievement will serve to provide the political leadership they need to influence others to follow. By itself, personal achievement usually *isn't* enough, except, perhaps, for the small circle of people closest to the leader. Achievement leaders must exert influence by building a community of achievers. This is accomplished by coaching, retraining, and rewarding those who can and will achieve, and replacing or removing those who can't or won't achieve.

The community of achievers is expanded by increasing the positive achievement leverage of the organization. When the behavior of achievers is reinforced, a magnet of accomplishment spirals out and grows. As it does, it attracts others to exercise their potential to achieve while repelling those who can't or won't achieve. As this process unfolds, nonachievers find themselves increasingly isolated and either leave on their own or are removed.

Develop the Three Paths of Achievement

Most of us end up following all three paths to achievement during our careers.

In the early years we usually follow the service path; in later years, when we have gained a lot of experience, we may follow the innovation path. Throughout, we must manage, whether that means self-management or the management of others. One person I have come to know very well took all these paths and remains, in my mind, a perfect model of achievement.

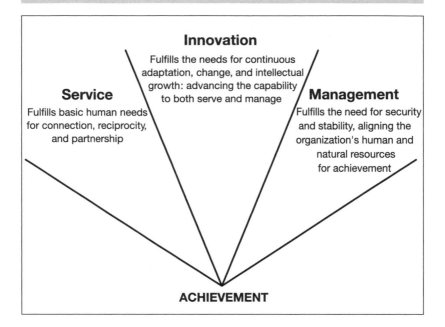

Marliese Hauptmann Mooney emigrated from Germany to the United States after World War II, initially finding work as a model in New York. She married an academic, and began raising five children while training and working as a nurse. Eventually she earned an MBA and served as a hospital CEO, a challenging job for a woman who became the sole provider for her family after the untimely death of her husband. Hauptmann Mooney became known as a no-nonsense leader of great personal integrity and was tapped by corporate health care for increasingly important roles, including her appointment as CEO of AMI, the largest international health-care consulting firm in the world.

Her first challenge arose just prior to her appointment, when the prime minister of Singapore asked for a very private meeting with her on his way back home from a state visit to Washington, D.C. At the Mooney home in Beverly Hills, the prime minister expressed his grave concerns about an infant slave trade cartel centered in Singapore. The most outrageous aspect of the enterprise was the surgical conversion of female infants into males to make them more marketable. He was concerned that unscrupulous surgeons were using AMI's hospital, among others, to conduct the operations.

Could she help, he asked? A constant practitioner of all Seven Principles of Achievement, Marliese postponed her public appointment as CEO and assigned herself as a staff surgical nurse in AMI's Singapore medical center. Challenged by her board chair regarding this decision, she told him, "If the other leaders of this company and I aren't willing to actually live up to our responsibilities in the frontlines of care, we don't belong here and, I assure you, those who don't, won't be!" Her response became legend when, after five long months, she initiated, with the prime minister's assistance, an international investigation by the United Nations and the governments of Singapore, China, and others that led to exposure and criminal conviction of slave trade ringleaders, including government officials in several countries.

Service. Innovation. Management. Marliese did it all. From her experiences as a child in war-torn Germany through her rise through the ranks of leadership, she dedicated her life to service. She sought innovative solutions to problems such as the infant slave trade crisis. And she distinguished herself as a manager all along the way.

These results of our Talent IQ research match the findings of such social theorists as David McClelland, among others, that societies, organizations, and individuals advance and decline as a result of how they choose to advance their power. If you opt to advance through affiliation (who you know), you will most likely prefer manipulation. If you choose to advance through power, you will likely substitute coercion, control, or tyranny for the sort of innovative problem-solving and coaching that characterizes good management.

Great organizations identify and select talent that can harness the Seven Principles of Achievement, create a magnet of achievement, and excel on the three paths to achievement. Let's turn our attention next to the critical topic of talent selection.

CHAPTER 2

Select Achievers

IMAGINE GETTING A late-night phone call from your boss; your assignment is the following: "I need you to identify the ideal characteristics of the Supreme Allied Commander of Europe. We are going to use the criteria you outline to benchmark how our top commanders measure up to those characteristics. Do this thoroughly and quickly. And, make sure you get input from FDR and Churchill. The outcome of World War II depends on this assignment."

Such was the call that Colonel Dwight Eisenhower received from General George Marshall—FDR's indispensable wartime architect. The characteristics Eisenhower identified proved prophetic. First, the supreme commander must be "his own man," a self-reliant achiever impervious to either manipulation or coercion. He had to be pragmatic and propose solutions that would work, as the Allied Forces could not afford to waste time or resources on vain gambles or territorial grabs for glory. Also, whomever was selected had to be willing to listen and learn quickly, yet remain steadfastly humble as he took responsibility for selecting and managing the talent it would take to win the war. He had to manage a diverse group of talented individuals—individuals who might be in a pressure-cooker situation. Whoever was named supreme commander would need to practice and promote partnership among all those who fought. Such a partnership required a commitment to stay the course, regardless of setbacks and obstacles, and a resolute optimism in the capacity of people to overcome any challenge. Most of all, the supreme commander must possess the courage to accept personal responsibility for the results every step of the way.

When Eisenhower outlined these characteristics to his boss, Marshall remarked that Eisenhower had grasped the gravity and opportunity of the role in its full complexity. "To what degree do our commanders display the characteristics? Whom do we select?" queried Marshall.

Eisenhower's answer has become legend, not only because of the decision it eventually sparked, but because of the more general insight it provided. "In all candor," Eisenhower responded, "I cannot find a satisfactory match. MacArthur is brilliant but vain and dogmatic. He will immediately alienate a dogmatic Montgomery, whose vanity equals and, if possible, exceeds his own. Alexander possesses the pragmatism and commitment, but he is tradition-bound to put England's national interests above those of the global partnership. Patton is a chivalric genius who believes a hammer blow solves all problems and Bradley presently lacks the personal achievement to assert his will and demand accountability."

Marshall agreed and instructed Eisenhower to make additional comparisons, this time with Eisenhower's name included. Marshall, of course, knew where the assignment would lead from the very beginning. Eisenhower did not. Had Eisenhower not gone through the rigorous identification and selection process, however, he may not have accepted the results: *he* displayed the best match. When Eisenhower reported the second assessment, Marshall told him he already knew the result. And, before Eisenhower could comment further, Marshall told him to accept selection as Supreme Allied Commander. History bears witness to the wisdom of that decision.

Make-or-Break Selection

Does your organization's selection process involve the explicit identification of attributes and the rigorous candidate-matching demanded by Marshall? Of the 964 organizations involved in our study, fewer than 6 percent did. Yet, those who did accounted for 55 percent of the highest achievers the study identified. Coincidence? Hardly. The combination of a disciplined protocol and a clear understanding of prized characteristics helped this small minority of organizations make the right make-or-break selection decisions.

Again, history proves the long-term value of effective selection. Eisenhower performed brilliantly as Supreme Allied Commander and went on to two terms as president. Marshall had known Eisenhower's selection was a make-or-break decision. Since Marshall himself could not take on the assignment, he resolved to select someone who could, and would, succeed. Interestingly, Marshall broke ranks for his selection, elevating Eisenhower, who was a mere colonel at the time, to four-star rank within two years. In the end, Marshall decided to let talent trump rank, tenure, and ego—a decision that could have been deleterious to morale.

However, more surprising than the decision itself was the response of the other Allied commanders who backed Marshall's selection with cooperation and commitment. Even the Caesar-like MacArthur was compelled to admit that Eisenhower possessed the tenacity and levelheadedness required of the job.

Marshall was a supreme pragmatist. He based his decision on achievement and fit. The criteria he used for selection were widely, if informally, disseminated so that those who might question the decision came to understand the complex and important reasons for his selection—and, most important, what would thus be expected of them.

Is selection in your organization handled with the same clear-headed discipline and pragmatism? If not, why not? How can you take action to make selection more effective?

Today's challenges require brilliant selection of talent. When it comes to building a great organization, selection is the seminal make-or-break decision. That's why the process should be rigorous, thorough, and carried out with the utmost commitment. As our research and experience demonstrates, the selection process in many organizations all too seldom receives the focus it requires, a crime for which companies can pay the price for years and years. Think of successful and failed organizations you've known. Their fate was invariably the result of selection and the talent management that followed.

Why Selection Fails

Given the critical nature of selection, and in light of the fact that most everyone at the very least pays lip service to its value, it's astonishing that senior leadership in many organizations so often abdicates responsibility for it. When this happens, "affiliators" will quickly install a group-think process in which the principal criteria for selection relate to a candidate's ability to "go along to get along."

"Power players," on the other hand, do the opposite, limiting the process to a tightly circumscribed list of functional criteria that channel the candidate into accepting a compliant and submissive posture from the very beginning of the working relationship. To avoid these pitfalls, achievement leaders must insist that objective achievement criteria guide the identification, selection, and reselection of candidates. If achievers allow affiliators and power players to rule the selection process, the organization is doomed.

A classic case involves IBM's failure to reassert achievement criteria during the 1970s and early 1980s when declining productivity, lagging innovation, and the inability to retain high-achieving employees plagued the computer giant. An incisive confidential study of the reasons for IBM's corporate decline, commissioned by then-CEO John Akers for the board, pinpointed the root cause as *the firm's failure to implement an achievement-driven identification, selection, and reselection—including evaluation—process*. This failure also explained a work force that was bloated by measurably poor performers. On a five-point scale, ranging from 1 for poor performance through fair, acceptable, above average, and up to 5 for superior performance, 15 percent of IBM employees ranked at a 1! (No company should ever exceed 2–3 percent of employees at that performance level.)

When critics assail the radical surgery performed under CEO Alan Gerstner in the 1980s and 1990s, they ignore how far IBM had strayed from its roots as a high-achieving organization. Instead, the *appearance* of class and success too often passed for the real thing. Informal quotas for the selection of candidates from the "right" schools became more important than finding candidates with the right skills and experience. Who you knew (affiliation) or who you could manipulate (power plays) would get you promoted faster than would your actual accomplishments.

The Three-Step Process

One of my early mentors, Dr. Franklin Berry, president of the President's Institute of the American Management Association, liked to tell CEOs: "Who is selected says who you are more than any other act of leadership. If you don't take charge of selection, and mean it, it is a gross abdication of responsibility for which you should be fired!" Dr. Berry, an otherwise soft-spoken man, pulled no punches on this issue. Neither did General Marshall in selecting Eisenhower as supreme commander, nor Gordon Moore in selecting Andy Grove as head of Intel, nor Reginald H. Jones in choosing Jack Welch to guide GE. Neither should you!

The process that great leaders and their organizations employ involves three steps:

31

Step 1	Identification
Step 2	Selection
Step 3	Reselection

Most managers and organizations are at least somewhat familiar with the first two of these steps, but falter when it comes to the third. What is reselection? Over time, the match between people and the work they do changes. As your company, industry, or the marketplace evolves, so will the requirements of each position in your organization. Talents, education, or skills that would have been "nice-to-haves" or not necessary when you initially hired for the position may now, in fact, be critical in order for the employee to achieve a base line of competence. Moreover, employee talents and skills can also be developed. Has the employee outgrown the position he or she is in? Any selection process should accommodate the need for realignment, advancement, and reassignment. And, while careful evaluation addresses many key issues, it should not replace a full-fledged reselection review. We'll cover this in more depth later in the chapter.

Step 1: Identification

Can you honestly say you include achievement characteristics as a formal part of your search and selection criteria? Typically, most organizations pay more attention to functional job descriptions, including technical, educational, and experiential criteria. Criteria related to important personal attributes, such as achievement, seldom receive the emphasis they deserve. Yet, we have found that those attributes account for 95 percent of both advancements and terminations.

Over the past 20 years or so, in particular, organizations have become gun-shy about specifying the attributes most essential to performance success. Why?

1. Failure to appreciate the importance of the hard-to-quantify factors that contribute to success and failure.
2. Fear of equal opportunity violations.
3. Apathy and bureaucratic processing.

We've seen the importance of the first reason in Chapter 1; let's look a little more closely at the latter two. Ironically, devotion to equal opportunity without emphasis on achievement actually promotes prejudice against our most diverse groups of workers. Latinos, Asians, African Americans, Eastern Europeans, and women share an overriding characteristic: a history of achieving despite adversity.

While the unexpectedly rapid decline of the domestic male advantage and the ascendance of women and minorities has transformed the job market into a more universally competitive one, failure to make achievement the centerpiece of selection will continue to invite poor results. From Franklin to Lincoln to Martin Luther King Jr., achievement has, more than anything else, accounted for pluralism's success. Here is where ideology and practice meet. If we are serious about pluralism, we must be serious about achievement and the focus on performance that follows.

The Consequences of Carrying Poor Performers

On a purely practical level, underemphasizing achievement prejudices selection in favor of choosing affiliators, those who "know the right people," or power players, those who will eagerly "comply and repay." As our research tellingly reveals, organizations populated with affiliators and power players decline and fail at an alarming rate. One simple way to determine the extent to which this situation happens in your organization is to ask if your high achievers feel they must compensate for or "carry" the poor-performing affiliators and power players. "Carrying" poor performers can destroy the motivation of achievers.

Test this finding in your own organization by conducting an informal poll among your best performers. Ask your top performers to identify the top three challenges or opportunities facing them in their work. If "compensation for poor performers or the results of their work" is listed more than 30 percent of the time among the top three challenges they face, then you've been infected by the virus of poor performers. Thirty percent represents a tipping point. Beyond it lies ruin. Whenever high performers report a 30 percent or greater "carrying" problem, the team in question will sooner or later suffer low profitability, poor quality, eroded customer satisfaction, and high turnover among the most talented people.

Poor performers cling to the legs of their desks, while the high performers who are burdened with carrying them look for desks elsewhere. In technical, professional, and health-care firms, we found these problems 1.5 times more likely to occur than in general business organizations. In the former, individual performance issues come more readily to the surface because "carrying" lackluster performers can make or break them in rather dramatic ways. In a hospital, for example, it is a matter of life and death. However, even if you make and sell toy airplanes, you should take this problem just as seriously—your survival in the marketplace may depend on it.

Apathy and Bureaucratic Processing

When you find too much "carrying" of underperformers going on, you almost always find the corollary of apathy and bureaucratic processing. One feeds the other. The failure to honor achievement inevitably cuts out operational leaders, those most responsible for performance in the frontlines of service. When this happens, apathy pollutes the whole selection process, turning it into a bureaucratic act of posting and filling jobs, where those involved in identification and selection, including interviewing, will never actually train or coach those selected. This, ultimately, produces a dangerous disconnect between what customers need—achievers who serve, innovate, and manage—and what those selected can and will do.

Identification in Action

To use the achievement profile in the actual selection process, you must appreciate the way it translates into specific patterns of behavior. The following Achievement in Action Grid helps to explain some of the ways achievers express their abilities while pursuing the three fundamental paths of action in organizational life: service, innovation, and management.

Achievement in Action Grid

Paths of Action

	Service	Innovation	Management
Responsibility	Hero - Achiever	Hero - Achiever	Hero - Achiever
Optimism	Guide	Discoverer	Problem Solver
Commitment	Benefactor	Empowerer	Guardian
Partnership	Empathizer	Knowledge Leader	Builder
Achievement (pragmatism and humility)	Engager	Seeker	Organizer

The 7 Principles of Achievement

You'll notice that this chart reverses the order of the Seven Principles of Achievement you saw in the Introduction and has clustered the first three (embrace achievement, be pragmatic, and practice humility) together at the bottom because the first three characteristics form the foundation of achievement and precede the major developmental stages of partnership, commitment, optimism, and responsibility. When we examine the work experience of achievers, we look to see how far along this maturational ladder of development they have progressed by looking at the extent to which we see expressions of achievement along the three primary paths of achievement—service, innovation, and management.

To review, *service* means reaching out to others to achieve the results through partnership. It can take the form of communication, networking, coaching, and relationship building, among others. *Innovation* means making discoveries, adapting to change, and then sharing those accomplishments. Such efforts range from scientific and medical breakthroughs to the development of innovative ways to solve problems, market products and services, finance growth, and invent new strategies for meeting the changing needs of your customer or the marketplace. Finally, *management* means mobilizing and aligning resources, including both people and materials, to meet the needs of others. Here, such issues as oversight, efficiency, productivity, compliance, and contract fulfillment dominate the agenda.

Each of the cells in the grid describes a trait displayed by an achiever on a particular path of work. For example, at the foundation level, those on the service path begin by making contact and *engaging* with others, be they teammates or customers. At the partnership level of service, the *Empathizer* "walks in the other's shoes," meaningfully grasping the other individual's real needs. At the commitment level of service, the *Benefactor* shares the burden and helps others confront and overcome the challenges they face. At the optimism level, the *Guide* takes the initiative to chart a specific course of direction. And, finally, at the responsibility level, the *Hero* inextricably ties his or her fate to the welfare of others, who, in turn, dedicate themselves to sharing the journey from the present state of life to a new and better one.

To serve will, of course, ultimately require a willingness and ability to innovate. On this path, the achiever progresses upward: *seeking* solutions, *acquiring* knowledge, and *discovering* new ideas and methods. This path, too, culminates in *empowering* others, before *achievement* is reached

Both service and innovation naturally require the ability to manage: *organizing* people and materials, *building* the infrastructure of mores and agreements that bind a community of people together, *guarding* and *protecting* the community, *solving* all the inevitable problems that may threaten stability and well-being. In the end, the achiever again reaches *hero-achiever* status.

Identifying the Hero in Each of Us

Few of us, of course, ever fully function at the level of hero, but, regardless of our position in an organization, each of us can perform heroically when we seize the opportunity to do so. Think of those who have mentored you and those who have helped your organization perform magnificently. Without a touch of heroism, none of this happens. And, without a willingness to identify, select, and reselect for the heroic, you will never find it.

Every work role includes aspects of all three paths to achievement, whether you work as a shipping clerk, a middle manager, or a CEO. The more you have matured along one path, the more you will develop skills along the others and/or understand the need to collaborate with associates who do achieve them. Paradoxically, the more TalentLeaders mature, the more they wish to share with others. This creates what we call the "Synergistic Kick," a turbocharging effort that moves an organization from merely good to great. When you've identified and selected TalentLeaders capable of the heroic, you have also planted the seeds of greatness for others.

Therefore, as you develop your Achievement in Action Grid for identification, ask yourself how you expect successful people to act as they pursue each path in the workplace. Think through the characteristics that identify the achievers you need for a particular role in your organization, and expand the range of terms already provided in each cell of the grid to target attributes as precisely as possible. The higher the level of a role's responsibility, the more likely you will find that it requires competencies in all three pathways of achievement. However, in most cases, individual roles will emphasize competencies along one pathway. Clearly identify required competencies to specify "must haves," "should haves," and "nice to haves." While any successful individual will learn how to stride along all of the paths, that person will most likely display the strongest skills along one pathway, especially in the beginning.

As you go through the selection step of the process, this approach will enable you to forecast how well a candidate's experiences and capabilities may translate into behaviors that greatly enhance your organization.

Step 2: Selection

While selection consists of many activities, such as formal tests, reference checks, and even background investigations, TalentLeaders focus on a carefully scripted face-to-face interviewing process. In the end, nothing can replace a probing, interactive dialogue in which both partners freely ask and answer questions. Ninety-nine percent of the top 5 percent of TalentLeaders in our study said they would never make a selection decision that lacks such a dialogue.

The selection script utilized overwhelmingly by the top TalentLeaders concentrates on work history, during which candidates walk through their career from the very first job they ever held to the present, noting the dates they started and stopped for each. Such a walk-through provides a "work-life map" that, by itself, affords you powerful insights into an individual's achievement history.

Of course, at each stop along the work-life journey, you can pause to probe and discuss personal idiosyncrasies, strengths and weaknesses, motivations and goals, and feelings about relationships. "What drew you to that job? What did you like or dislike about it? What did you learn from it? What successful relationships did you develop? Can you recall any unsuccessful relationships?" Always conduct such interviews in a private, nonthreatening setting and act as an empathic listener, spending approximately 75 percent of the interview time questioning and probing. Let's see how this works in actual practice.

Case Study: Selecting a CEO

The Hospital Corporation of America was searching for a CEO for its international subsidiary, HCA United Kingdom and Europe.

This extremely prestigious position offered such an unprecedented opportunity for growth that it demanded the utmost care in accurately identifying and selecting just the right person. Among the board responsible for the process, one cluster of opinion centered on the need for a broadly and deeply connected candidate: "Someone who can personally invite Margaret Thatcher to tea," as one board member, a member of the Washington, D.C. elite, noted. Another school of thought emphasized immediate return on investment: "Where are the profits? The ventures with Cambridge University and the Vatican sound really good. But, we need someone who will 'show us the money,'" insisted the chairman and CEO of a leading investment firm. Still another focused on building it right: "We've passed $400 million in revenue despite less than stellar leadership. Now we need someone who believes in the opportunities private health care can offer and knows how to make it happen in cultures with no experience with it." "We want a CEO with great initiative, creativity, and commitment," said another board member, a chairman and CEO of a major U.S. bank.

As the discussion heated up, I suggested that the board "weight" their requirements as percentages. "Of 100 percent, what percent of success came about through networking, what percent by immediate productivity and profit generation, and what percent by growth and development? To help you craft those numbers, ask yourselves which attributes cannot be purchased or delegated but must reside in the CEO."

An intense and freewheeling discussion ensued. "Well, we know we can make the connections with lobbyists. And, several of us have connections that can get the CEO started," said the proponent of tea with Thatcher. "Yes, but we'd better start seeing some cash flow pretty soon or the whole venture will be at risk," responded another. This led to a rapid-fire sequence of responses: "But, if the pressure for profits undermines long-term value, we could compromise our investment." "Hey, we're still ahead of the profit curve we promised shareholders, so let's not panic." "Yes, and we're finally gaining the credibility essential to attract exceptional physicians. Just look at the university medical faculty practicing at our Cambridge facility."

"Which brings us back to the core question," responded the founder and first CEO of HCA, Dr. Tom Frist Sr. "Whomever we select must be someone with tremendous competence, a person of great personal initiative and commitment—both to private care and to seeing that patients get only the best care possible. He must be able to think on his feet, to adapt and respond to changing circumstances and opportunities quickly. And, he must be responsible. Someone in whose hands you could trust your life . . . and your wallet."

Dr. Frist Sr. summed it up nicely. To push the exercise forward to the numbers, the board then voted on the weighting: 60 percent to the knowledgeable, committed adapter; 20 percent to the networker; and 20 percent to the "immediate" profit generator. The next step, everyone agreed, was to delegate a specific subcommittee that was to break down the general attributes into specific characteristics before launching the ultimate search.

Eventually, the search committee nominated four strong candidates, three thoroughbreds and one dark horse. It seemed that every candidate with some measure of "pull" had applied, and three of them had made it into the final four. Although they presented flawless credentials, none matched the identification criteria as well as the board hoped they would. Two were great networkers who knew practically everybody there was to know. Both came from world-renowned hospitals, but, when it came to how health care worked, one said he'd create an open-door policy to inspire harmony and understanding. He meant that literally, citing his practice of removing his office door and hanging it from the ceiling to signal his openness. The other thought that the "messy" stuff should be left to those who lacked the ability to understand the higher needs of health care.

As I probed their work histories, neither reported much work experience before leaving graduate school. And, while both were very bright, neither had ever struggled to land a job. They both started out at their alma mater's teaching hospital and went from one very strong organization to another, where they essentially played the part of board luncheon companion and gopher.

The third candidate was a take-no-prisoners leader who was extremely bright and talented, but who had gained his reputation as a health-care entrepreneur by putting together deals in which, in retrospect, the human chemistry did not coalesce. When I asked him about this perception, he responded, "People go where you make it impossible not to go. I basically say, here's where the opportunity is. Take it, or leave it. Literally." That left the fourth candidate, the dark horse, Chuck Newman.

I asked Chuck the same question I had asked all the others: "Can you tell me about the first job you ever held?" He paused, then said, "Well, in college, I . . ." I interrupted him immediately. "Excuse me, I meant your very first job." "Well, in high school . . ." I interrupted him again. "Was that your very first job?" And so it went until Chuck replied, "I guess I was seven when I took over a paper route. I didn't understand what I was doing and how much work it took. But, I stuck it out for five years and grew it to 145 customers, 160 on Sundays. Along the way, I hired other guys off and on to help me. Then, I sold it to an older kid for $100 when I took another job helping my neighbor's brother in landscaping." "And, when was that?" I asked. "What year and month did you start the landscaping job?"

And so it went. For every significant job in Chuck's history, I asked him when he took it, when he left it, and why. Gradually, a picture emerged of someone who had acquired an in-depth understanding of what it took to take the initiative at quite an early age. However, the work-life history also revealed that Chuck had suffered a very serious disruption during his transition from high school to the University of Michigan, to which he had won a full scholarship.

When I asked him about specific studies and results in high school, a legitimate part of everyone's job history, Chuck replied that his last semester had been a nightmare. His mother had become seriously ill and subsequently passed away. Though it would have been unethical and insensitive for me to probe that tragedy directly, as we discussed his transition from high school, Chuck volunteered that he just did not have the "heart" for college and, somewhat on the spur of the moment, joined the army. He subsequently became a medic and served two tours in Vietnam in the frontlines, where he received commendations for bravery.

As we followed the path of his work history, there emerged the pattern of someone who cared deeply and took initiative—occasionally impetuously, but nevertheless, with the intelligence and resolve to adapt successfully when presented with challenges. As you might expect from a man with such character, Chuck returned from Vietnam, enrolled in college, and went straight through to his MBA. Upon graduation he immediately joined HCA, where he had served successfully in increasingly more responsible, and difficult, roles, culminating in his position as district vice president overseeing ten hospitals and academic teaching centers with combined revenues in excess of $600 million. At thirty-seven, he had progressed far and fast and had earned a reputation as a tireless executive deeply dedicated to health care and the patients it served.

Was he mature enough to handle a job as prominent as CEO of HCA United Kingdom and Europe? A big part of the answer came when I asked him what his experience as a medic had taught him. "I learned that suffering is something all of us will endure at some point," he answered, without skipping a beat. "However, not all of us will have somebody there who really cares and who can help us through it. In a very real way, when I helped troops in the field, they helped me heal. I won't ever forget that or what it takes to do health care right."

The rest of the answer came when I asked him why he wanted to be CEO. His answer revealed another aspect of his executive character: "I don't want to have 'tea with Thatcher.' I want to grow HCA's international operations and have a real impact on advancing the concept that everyone should have access to private care. And, I want to learn a lot and make lifelong friends in the process."

When I reported to the board and recommended Chuck for the job, I mentioned the "tea with Thatcher" comment. "Anyone with his background and priorities gets my vote." The board member who had first brought up "tea with Thatcher" agreed. So did everyone else. How did Chuck do? He tripled the size of the company in four years and set unprecedented records for profitability and, most important, patient satisfaction.

Not every selection turns out as well as this one, but the odds of success greatly increase when you reduce the risk of failure by following a protocol that gets to the core of a person's competencies and character. The board chose an achiever and got results beyond its expectations.

The Strategic Key to Selection

Developing insight into a person's work-life history is the key strategy behind successful selection interviewing. While other aspects are important, including the private, face-to-face collegial setting, everything else is of less importance than understanding the actual experiences of a person's work life. And, since we spend the better part of our lives working, a person's work-life history provides profound insight into a person's motivations, discipline, flexibility, personal tolerance or biases, fears and hopes, and ability to perform.

From a candidate's point of view, being asked to share one's work-life history is either a great opportunity or a threat. For achievers, the opportunity to share one's work-life history is a privilege and a courtesy they will never forget. While they are aware that such an interviewing strategy will expose their failures, they see this as an opportunity, not a threat. For them, overcoming failure and adversity are central to their identity and a reason for personal and professional success. They want you to know these are the values they hold and how they acquired them.

By contrast, affiliators and power players do not usually welcome a work-life history. They'd rather tell you about who they know or how they've powered their way up the ladder. A work-life history will reveal the reasons they've become affiliators or power brokers and why they are likely to be a performance risk.

More than any other aspect of the selection interview, developing an in-depth understanding of a candidate's work-life history is the key to success.

Step 3: Reselection

Reselection is the most underappreciated aspect of managing talent-on-the-bubble. Reselection has not received sufficient attention because many leaders assume that if they hire the right person, achievement will follow. It may or may not. Therefore, leaders should constantly ask whether staff members are properly aligned and motivated. Are they working in the right role, with the right set of responsibilities to achieve the mission of the organization? Too often, new managers who have recently assumed responsibility for a new group, or long-term managers who have not focused on their team for some time, may fail to recognize how circumstances have changed in ways that have caused misalignment of people.

In such situations you should conduct a reselection interview with individual team members. Ask for an opportunity to "get to know" your team members, or, for established relationships, to get reacquainted. You want to understand how associates on your team fit with present challenges. First, reapply the Achievement in Action Grid. Where does each person stand on the three paths? Then conduct a slightly modified selection interview. Again, the key is the work-life script. See the following case study for an example.

Case Study: Reggie Gruber

I have drawn this case from a situation that could have resulted in tragedy if we had not conducted an effective reselection interview.

The details have been changed to protect the innocent (and the guilty).

Dennis Walters was preparing to take over the family business, a multistate retail lighting and contracting company, from his father, Ted. Dennis had asked me to advise him on an unpleasant matter: getting rid of a once-valuable but now unproductive individual in their organization. As Dennis told me, "Look, Emmett, I'm determined to clean house, and I'm going to start by getting rid of some dead wood—like Reggie. You know she's been with Dad from the beginning. And, yes, she got me started here. But, as VP of marketing, she's a disaster. She's got to go!" Rather than green-lighting the removal of Reggie Gruber, however, I strongly recommended a reselection process.

Dennis was smart, experienced, and aggressive. He was also stubborn once he'd formed an opinion—and, in his opinion, Reggie would have to go, regardless of what he learned from the reselection interview with her. Dennis's dad, Ted Walters, did, indeed, want to see Dennis take over, but in a way that would not send the company's culture and customers into a tailspin. As Ted confided in me, "How can we help Dennis grow and develop a deeper understanding of people and their needs? He can be a loose cannon, and I'm afraid he'll sink the ship if he doesn't learn a little flexibility and humility." I suggested that Dennis join me in key interviews so I could maximize his learning and eliminate any destructive behavior.

Dennis and I met with Reggie in a comfortable conference room where the sales managers often entertained major customers. "Reggie," I began, "thank you for joining Dennis and me. Would it be all right if we set aside discussion of marketing and sales issues for the moment and, instead, asked you to share your work history with us? I understand you've played an important role here for some time."

Reggie seemed surprised by that question. Perhaps she had been steeling herself for a head-on collision with Dennis. However, she smiled at my compliment and said, "Sure, Dr. Murphy. In fact, I would very much appreciate that opportunity. I know we're here to discuss my performance, and I think we should. But, I also think it's important to understand who I am and how I can contribute to this company."

One of the key lessons in humility that everyone who conducts reselection interviews learns is that colleagues usually understand what's going on with them and the organization. They don't fear honest discussion as much as they fear the unknown. Reggie would eagerly share her experiences with us and, in the process, willingly engage in finding a solution to her present challenges.

You'll recognize this script. "Reggie, will you tell us about the first job you ever held?" I asked. "Well," she responded, "when I was twenty . . ." I interrupted. "Excuse me, Reggie, but I mean the *very* first job." We repeated this dance two more times before Reggie said, "Oh, I get it!" Then she walked us through a work-life history that gave insights we could have gotten no other way.

Reggie, the oldest of four, with two brothers and one sister, was orphaned when she was five years old. After her parents were killed in a car accident, family members and friends raised the four children in a rural community. Her *first* job? Feeding chickens and cows on the farm where she stayed. Survival depended on earning her keep. Amazingly, from the outset, she managed to save money. Despite her age, she still felt responsible to do all she could to take care of her siblings. She did this so well that she eventually put two through college, and one through medical school.

By age eight she went to another farm, where she could earn more. By twelve, she was working part-time at a farmer's market; by fourteen she ran the produce section at a local grocery store; by seventeen she became the night manager and dropped out of high school. An exceptionally bright student, she nevertheless put her education on hold, and by nineteen she moved up to store manager. Then she began taking a few courses at a community college, where she met her future husband. As she progressed in college, she won promotion to district manager, a position that put her in touch with Ted Walters when she negotiated a contract with him.

Five years later, having finished her baccalaureate and delivered the third of her five children, she joined Ted. From there, she says, she spent thirty-four years working her way up from the docks, to the counter, to floor sales, to retail management, financial management, VP of operations and, presently, VP of marketing.

"That is an extraordinary career," I said. "May I ask, when you look back over your career, how do you feel?" I'll never forget Reggie's answer, and neither will Dennis.

"I feel proud, but tired," she said. "Right now, I'm disappointed in my performance as VP of marketing. Someone with more capability and miles on the tires should be in this role. I'm too grateful to Ted and too committed to Dennis not to want to see the best person in this role. I know it's not me."

"That's a generous and gracious analysis," I responded. "But, what do you think you should be doing?"

She had obviously been thinking about this question long before I asked it. "I should be back on the counter providing support to any and all who need it. I would like to give back to this company something of what it has given to me and my family. And, I can do that best by taking a reassignment, at the pay grade counter people receive. That's what I would like to do."

In the end, Dennis learned a priceless lesson in humility and humanity, Reggie went to work in a job that helped all her colleagues, and the company's culture and customers benefited as well. The decision signaled to the whole organization that the passing of the baton from Ted to Dennis would not damage the fundamental culture and mission that had long marked the organization as a wonderful place to work and be served.

The Strategic Key to Reselection

We all grow and change. TalentLeaders want to share how they've grown and changed. They want to contribute. They want to be "all they can be."

High-achieving leaders understand this need because they see it in themselves. That is why asking subordinates for the opportunity to review their work-life history is so important. Just as the work-life history drives the initial selection interview, it also drives the reselection and review process. Every leader has both the obligation and right to understand the talent resources at hand. Asking subordinates for the opportunity to review their work-life history creates an opportunity achievers will value.

One of the best ways to conduct a reselection interview is to call it a "getting acquainted or reacquainted" session. Once a leader establishes these sessions as part of his or her normal practice, subordinates react responsively. The best way to initiate the practice is to start with several high performers to establish a positive tone. Then, a leader can move through the rest of the staff in a more or less random manner.

The Work-Life Interview Script

As you've seen with both Chuck and Reggie, the most basic part of the work-life script is "What was the first job you ever held?" Leaders are often puzzled by the simplicity of this question until they go through an interview driven by this question and its corollaries themselves. While we couldn't explore all the corollaries in these case studies, they follow a logic flow that is driven by the principle that issues and experiences relevant to work history are open for discussion. Here's a sample flow of questions.

"What was your very first job? When did you take it? Why did you take it? When did you leave it? Why? When did you start your next job? Why did you take the position? What did you learn? What were your most memorable experiences? What did you like about it? Why? What did you not like about it? Why? How closely did you work with others on the job? With your boss? When did you leave? Why? When did you start your next job? Why did you take it?" If there was a gap between jobs, ask: "May I ask what you did between the time you left one job and took the next? When did you leave that job? Why?" And so forth.

Note that it is important to maintain a consistent flow in your questioning. This is not a criminal inquiry like those on television or in the movies. While a work-life history script is designed to probe beneath the surface of the resume, it is also designed to help the interviewee think clearly and linearly.

Once you've gone through the linear portion of the script, you can now go back to key junctures and ask more probing intuitive and relationship questions, such as these: "Please tell me more about what you liked and disliked about your third job at XYZ Corporation. What gave you satisfaction, fulfillment, a sense of accomplishment? What got in the way of accomplishing what you most desired to do? What would you say were your greatest contributions? What were the areas in which you feel you may have fallen short?"

To the extent that questions related to work are appropriate, questions regarding personal matters away from work are not. The exception to this is when, for matters of security or safety, as spelled out ahead of time by the interviewer as relevant to job responsibilities, personal questions must be asked. In such cases, a security review usually follows the interview.

Why not ask personal questions? The first answer that comes to mind is that it is unethical and even illegal to do so. However, there are far more pragmatic and idealistic reasons. A leader needs to honor and respect a candidate or subordinate as much as he or she needs to search for information, if not more so. The questions a leader asks communicate, to both the subject and to others, what the leader stands for. If a leader stands for achievement, then questions will focus on work history. If a leader stands for other than achievement, it will be reflected in the nature of his or her questions and the dignity and integrity, or lack thereof, brought to the interviewing process.

In this context, the reselection process can have a dramatic effect on the morale of the whole team. If it is based on the work-life script and carried out with scrupulous attention to the issues of respect for subordinates as well as forthrightness and clarity in exercising leadership responsibility, it can have an extraordinarily positive and immediate impact. The opposite is also true.

However, to avoid the responsibility of reselection is to expose a leader to the even greater risk of being classified as a coward. A leader who avoids reselection and other such responsibilities abdicates responsibility for providing guidance and direction. He or she thus consigns the team to the whims of fate, where chaos reigns. Reselection sends the signal that "we will navigate a course to success together."

The work-life script will, of course, not only lead to the identification of achievers but also to those we refer to in this book as "talent-on-the-bubble." What do you do when you discover that someone is on-the-bubble? The answer is that you intervene. Your purpose in conducting the interview is to identify the strengths and weaknesses of your talent resources—your team. Just as an athletic coach or academic teacher should not hesitate to counsel or prescribe specific skills or communication training so, too, a leader assumes the roles of teacher, healer, and relationship builder, among others. Specific techniques for carrying out these roles are the subject of the rest of the book. The purpose of the work-life reselection script is to provide a leader with the diagnostic insight necessary to understanding what leadership role is required.

In the next two chapters, we'll explore two of these leadership roles—that of the coach, who maximizes achievement potentials, and that of the risk manager, who addresses talent-on-the-bubble.

CHAPTER 3

Coach for Achievement

GREAT COACHES WORK to accelerate the learning curve for talented people. They pay particular attention to talent-on-the-bubble in an effort to lead these individuals to greater levels of achievement. The sooner you can focus talented but misaligned people on mission-crucial work, the sooner your company gains a competitive advantage. On-the-job performance coaching can make that happen.

Whether provided by a direct superior or a specialist, effective coaching balances emphasis on the mental and the physical. Good coaches employ a continuous process of:

- Assessment and Planning
- Action
- Evaluation

Assessment and Planning

I had taken on a consulting engagement for Jerry Heims, co-founder of Kotak and Heims, a company Jerry and his late partner had grown from a small fish market to an $800 million regional food distributor. Now, the company was in trouble. It was neither big enough to leverage efficiencies of scale nor profitable enough to buy its way into the really big time. In an industry that measured success in terms of 1 percent to 2 percent margins, scale could mean everything. Increasingly, it seemed that only the sale of the company to a bigger player in the industry could protect family assets and the jobs of people Jerry valued as much as family.

He had asked his daughter Sonja Heims to come home and run the company. "I need someone I can truly trust," he explained to me. "But I need you to help her out, to get her ready for when I start stepping aside." Sonja was extremely talented. After working at a variety of low-level jobs at Kotak and Heims from fifth grade through summers and vacations home from college, she had secured a Stanford MBA and master's degree in economics before joining a Big Four accounting firm. She had risen to full partner, specializing in mergers and acquisitions. However, while I could see how her skills could help complete a successful merger, I couldn't quite see her actually operating Kotak and Heims.

The first step in the coaching process is to undertake an assessment of both the organizational context in which a subject is or will be working, and then, of the subject himself or herself. One of the most important findings of the Talent IQ research was the importance of grounding an individual's coaching in the reality of his or her organizational responsibilities. Thus, a coach must understand what an organization is going through and what it needs from the individual to be coached.

Understanding the realities facing the company provides a baseline for assessing the goodness-of-fit of the coaching subject. As you will see, we found that an in-depth application of the selection/reselection interview protocol combined with an assessment of problem-solving abilities and learning styles provides a very compelling picture of a subject's strengths and weaknesses. This picture can then be compared to the base line of corporate realities to diagnose the threats and opportunities facing the subject.

The diagnosis then provides a prescriptive framework for identifying the activities that should go into a coaching plan, including the priorities, deadlines, and implications for action. Such a process provides an efficient, pragmatic, and service-focused approach that can be adapted to a wide variety of settings. In a situation where the challenge is less intense, more emphasis can be placed on longer-term development and problem-solving, including more in-depth and targeted self-assessments. In more urgent situations, such as the one facing Sonja Heims in our case study, the process provides a protocol for rapid response and incisive intervention.

At the time, the company faced some critical short-term crises. AFL-CIO Union 1199 shop stewards had alleged that two deaths in the warehouse, due to falling shelves, might have been more than an accident and might instead have been the result of racial conflicts between the drivers and the warehouse workers. Tension was rife.

What had always been a calm and cooperative workplace now stood on the brink of civil war. Jerry knew he needed help. Rather than turn to an outsider to take the reins of president and chief operating officer, Jerry decided to recruit an adored family member.

The Coaching Imperative

To his credit, Jerry knew that his choice of a leader, and what he or she could achieve, would make or break the company. He also knew that his own existing skills would not suffice. Sonja, on the other hand, might possess the basic requisite skills, but bringing them up to speed would take control and *swift* coaching.

The new president and COO would have to be a performer from day one of the job. While Jerry longed for an immediate infusion of leadership energy and insight, he could not afford the risks inherent in learning on the job. To mitigate those risks, I suggested an immediate coaching marathon. The objective was to help Sonja focus on the most pressing company challenges and

53

future possibilities (such as exploring mergers), and to enable her to hone operation skills normally learned by trial and error. This case illustrates the coaching imperative.

You should undertake coaching within the context of a real and definable performance need.

Too often, managers think of it as a career development exercise disconnected from the immediate and pressing needs of the business. That is career counseling, *not* coaching. For coaching to succeed, you must clearly define the reason for undertaking it, take action, and measure results in terms of that reason. Coaching involves a real-world, real-time exercise in performance improvement that usually allows you to measure results fairly quickly, though hopefully not in the emergency mode in which Sonja would need to get them.

Know for Whom You Coach

Coaching requires a clear path of accountability. While Jerry had asked me to commit myself to Sonja's growth and development, I could not begin until we clarified a critical point.

"Jerry," I said, "I will certainly do all I can to help Sonja succeed, but I work for and report to *you*. You are the CEO; the company's fate is still in your hands. While I know you would like to step aside, you know you can't do that—yet. And, while we must move quickly and incisively, we must not skip or abort protocol. In fact, we must do just the opposite. This make-or-break-the-company effort must be done right. Fast, yes. But, right."

Although coaching certainly does aim to improve an individual's performance and skills, it must, first and foremost, support the organization's goals.

From the start, it requires a clear reporting relationship. Otherwise, coaching can become a loose cannon on deck, potentially aiming anywhere and everywhere but at mission targets. Given the fact that no tool can better maximize talent achievement, you must exercise care that coaching does not do more harm than good.

Our survey revealed that under no circumstances did Talent-Leaders believe in coaching without a mission-specific objective and clear path of accountability. If such an objective and path do not exist, forget coaching. Otherwise, you run the risk of indulging in a talented and ambitious person's narcissistic career objectives disconnected from the core mission of the company. In the case of "removal," superiors sometimes employ coaching for a person tracked for dismissal or to whom they wish to give "one last chance." Again, this doesn't call for coaching; it calls for counseling or outplacement, neither of which address immediate performance in the frontlines of your organization.

Coach Achievers

Meanwhile, back at Kotak and Heims, I continued with Sonja's father. "Jerry, while I know you have placed justified confidence in Sonja, I need to do my job and establish that she merits the coaching investment. You and those who depend on you, including your investors and bankers, have a right and responsibility to select the best available person, someone with a demonstrable work history of achievement and responsibility. Let's do this right, okay, and start at square one."

It's easy to confuse the speed of the times with the need for hastiness in decision-making. "Fast" can become a synonym for "careless." Think of a superb trauma surgeon or ER physician. Because she follows well-defined protocols for diagnosis, she can make both fast and responsible decisions. The same applies to talent coaching. We needed to clearly establish that Sonja could rise to the challenge—for her welfare as well as for the sake of the company.

55

Conduct a Selection Interview

I've chosen the ongoing Kotak and Heims case study for this chapter because it so clearly illustrates not only what happens in closely held or often family-run businesses, but also in publicly held businesses, where leaders can lock themselves into considering only candidates from the "company family." While most successful leaders do emerge from cultures where they have been developed for advancement, the most disastrous advancements result from "automatic, bureaucratic selections" where the goodness of fit and a history of appropriate achievement have fallen under the pressure of convenience and routine. Jerry agreed that we would not make that mistake here.

It took little persuading to bring Sonja "home" to Kotak and Heims. A born risk-taker, she loved her father and looked forward to, as she put it, "spreading her wings." However, her first stop was not the corporate headquarters, but my office, where I would conduct the first coaching interview in his presence. I wanted Jerry to witness firsthand his daughter's interview as a candidate, not as a family member. After introductions, I asked Sonja to walk us through her work history as if we had never met her before. She responded eagerly, as all achievers do.

Most achievers, especially those who emerge from cultures where they have enjoyed respect and rewards, fear that outsiders will not afford them the opportunity to tell their stories of achievement. Thus they jump at the chance to unfold their work-life histories. Those who have been languishing in affiliative and power player cultures tend to have left their jobs because they felt they had been denied the opportunity to compete openly for advancement. In the old environment, no one really cared to have them walk through their individual work history. They, too, delight in the chance to "strut their stuff."

Of course, I took it as a promising sign that Sonja was so excited about the opportunity and threw herself into the exercise with enthusiasm. The history she recounted impressed me even more because it both confirmed the CEO's (her father's) confidence, and it revealed the "fatal terrain" (a term that will be defined shortly) on which she could fail.

Having grown up working at an assortment of jobs at Kotak and Heims, Sonja understood most departments and functions pretty well except for that of the truck drivers, a constituency with which she would have to deal effectively. It would take more than her academic credentials and her success at a Big Four accounting firm to meet that and all the other challenges threatening the company.

How prepared was she, I asked, to meet these immediate challenges? While her early background spoke to her achievement ethic, her graduate education and professional experience raised questions about her potential distance from the present realities of the business and, perhaps, could have created an overconfidence in her own knowledge and skill. As it turned out, however, I needn't have worried.

"Frankly, it scares me," she responded. "After Dad phoned me and explained things, I called Gary [their corporate attorney and a colleague of mine], who helped flesh out the picture. This is a very complex and emotional environment. I'm not sure people realize how financially close to the edge the company is. Net value, as well as jobs, can go south pretty quickly. While I'm confident in what I've learned, I'll admit I'm not confident I have the answers for what we face here and now. That being said, there's too much at stake for all of us to let things deteriorate further. Quite honestly, I can't stand the thought of playing observer and letting that happen. So, ready or not, if you think I should, I'll give it a try." To Sonja's credit, she knew she did not know all the answers, but she felt confident she could find them. Of all the characteristics of achievers, none signals readiness for significant growth more clearly than strategic humility. Add to that her track record of initiative, service focus, commitment, hopefulness and, most important, a deep sense of responsibility. We offered her the job that very afternoon. Then, because she dove into the deep end, we embarked on the next phase of coaching, a rugged test of her problem-solving skills.

Assess Problem-Solving Skills

Recent research in cognitive and neuropsychology confirms the practical wisdom displayed by the TalentLeaders in our study. They understand that *how* you approach a problem or decision will determine, in large measure, whether or not your ultimate decision will get results. Why? Because your methodology will dictate what information you will gather and consider, how much weight you will give it in making your decision, and how much risk you will incur by not recognizing which information you may have missed.

Problem-Solving Styles

Analytical	Rational, linear, structured thinker; loves objective and hard data; focused on the present
Intuitive	Big picture, freeform, and nonlinear thinker; rational, conceptualizer, visionary, long-range thinker
Functional	Linear but also emotional; places high value on planning, organizing, and controlling; very pragmatic and goal-oriented
Personal	Emotional, freeform, and nonlinear thinker; places high value on sensitivity and interpersonal connection; enjoys the company of others

While you could consider literally thousands of factors when coaching someone, two should command your utmost attention: a person's history of achievement and the way he or she approaches problem-solving.

While a person's achievement history addresses questions of character, values, knowledge, and industriousness, methods of problem-solving reveal likely strengths and weaknesses when it comes to translating past achievement into future action.

A focus on achievement and problem-solving should govern the coaching process plan. It's a case of less is more. The more complicated the person and the responsibilities that he or she faces, the more simply and directly you should explore harnessing that individual's talent and energy.

When you examine a broad array of factors, you tend to look at each of them too superficially, obscuring a clear picture of a person's competence. Further, how the factors interrelate typically consumes more discussion time than does coaching a person's actual performance. Remember, in coaching, as in virtually all things, complexity added to complexity equals chaos.

To help direct our discussion, I asked Sonja to complete our proprietary TalentLeader Problem-Solving Inventory (PSI), which is a detailed self-assessment survey we developed as an outgrowth of our TalentLeader research. The PSI shows the individual problem-solving style and the extent to which a person approaches decision-making and problem-solving personally, functionally, personally, or intuitively.

Most of us don't see ourselves as clearly as others do. Ask friends, family members, colleagues, mentors, coaches, superiors, or people you manage to rate you with respect to each style (scoring 4 for high, 1 for low). You can place scores in the four quadrants of the Problem-Solving Inventory Map, located on the following page.

Problem-Solving Inventory Map

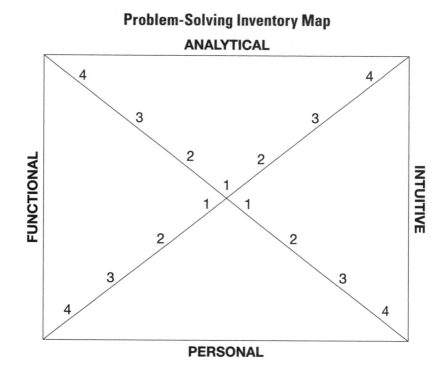

Whether rating yourself or someone else, look at several different problems. In Sonja's case, I asked her, with her father's input, to rate herself on four major decisions—choosing an MBA program, going to work for a Big Four accounting firm, buying her new Volvo, and deciding to accept her new job. Her answers are as follows:

"*I looked at three MBA programs, comparing costs, reputation, range of courses, professors, all the objective factors, though I'd say Stanford also appealed to me because of its location.*" That earned her a 3.5 analytical, 0.5 intuitive. "*My job? I wanted a big company where I could learn a lot of different skills. I also wanted to get back to the East Coast. They recruited me hard, and that was flattering.*" Here, she scored a 3 on functional, and 2 on personal. "*I bought a Volvo because it's a safe car. I read all the consumer reports. Plus I liked its conservative look.*" 3.5 analytical, 0.5 intuitive. "*Coming back home was 50 percent head and 50 percent heart, I've got to admit.*" So we gave her a 1 in each quadrant.

Here's Sonja's map:

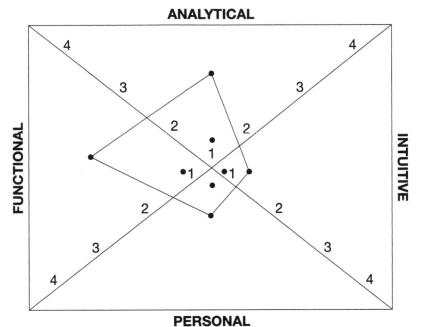

Clearly, Sonja strongly favored analytical and functional over personal and intuitive.

I summarized our findings. "Sonja, as you see, the PSI results suggest that you prefer to look at problems analytically. You also have a strong tendency to want to take charge and define objectives and outcomes clearly. While you are somewhat sensitive to relationships and personal perspectives, your primary concern when approaching a problem or decision is to gather information rationally in order to establish clear parameters for control. Would you say that's a reasonably accurate description of how you work?"

"Well, yes," she answered, "though I do think I'm a sensitive and imaginative person."

"I'm sure you are," I replied. "But, when it comes to solving a serious problem on the job, on what will you ultimately base your decision?" I asked.

"Okay. I see your point," she responded. "I like objective, measurable data that gives me a concrete sense of control."

"And, what kind of data and control do you have in this situation?"

"Well, the financial data is very straightforward and scary. And, as far as control, something is undermining it in an alarming way. From the financials and the description Bob and Dad gave me, the situation feels like quicksand."

"I can understand why you feel that way," I said. "Do you think collecting more financial data or immediately imposing some controls will work in this situation?"

"I don't know. But, I sure would be tempted to try to do both, and right away."

"What would make you hesitate doing that?" I asked. "What does your PSI map suggest regarding your risk in doing so?"

"Isn't it obvious? I haven't considered the personal side sufficiently, and I'm not even sure what the intuitive dimension even means."

Bravo! She was getting it. Could she add new arrows to her quiver? We'd see.

Identify "Fatal Terrain"

Sonja had demonstrated a significant degree of strategic humility in recognizing deficiencies in the scope of her problem-solving. But, such recognition by itself is not sufficient to change behavior related to the achievement of specific responsibilities. Sonja needed to understand that her deficiencies signaled the presence of a "fatal terrain" on which her leadership could fail.

Military analysts speak of the "fatal terrain" as that point on the map where a military force is most vulnerable for attack. Typically, it is an area that emphasizes the weaknesses of an enemy, one that stretches their knowledge, preparation, technology, and skills to the limit.

For Sonja, the fatal terrain was her lack of skills and understanding of the cultural and personal side of life at Kotak and Heims. The PSI had helped us identify where Sonja was most vulnerable for both an attack and self-destruction.

Whenever the fatal terrain is identified, it is critically important both to recognize its potential risk and to immediately take action to reduce it. For Sonja, failure to understand the environment that was producing labor strife and customer dissatisfaction could prove more dangerous to company survival than was declining profitability.

Thus, I told her that "everyone has a fatal terrain, an area where they are particularly vulnerable and exposed. The PSI suggests that yours could be a failure to consider the impact of culture and relationships on the present situation. You may also need to listen more closely to your intuition, how you feel about what's going to really make a difference. This vital dimension of thought can help pull together seemingly disconnected data, experiences, and ideas and reveal how they may affect outcomes."

The PSI can quickly lead to candid and pragmatic discussions of strengths and weaknesses, opportunities and threats. On-the-job coaching such as this will assist someone in harnessing their talent more fully to achieve positive results. An exclusive emphasis on a person's strengths can leave them fatally exposed by the weaknesses they would rather ignore.

Letting someone go forward without a thorough discussion of adding new strengths to his or her repertoire, or strengthening weaknesses, represents a coaching betrayal. It invites failure, failure that will reverberate in such destructive ways that it may cause permanent damage. In Sonja's case, such a failure could spell the end of the company.

Before we proceeded further in discussing the first steps of an action plan, I thought it would be helpful for Sonja to look at how her predecessor approached problem-solving. Earlier I had walked Jerry through four major decisions he had made: (1) growing his business, (2) deciding to retire, (3) bringing back Sonja, and

(4) buying a retirement home in Florida. For #1, he scored high on functional, low on intuitive; for #2, he scored high on personal; on #3 he scored ½ functional, ½ personal; and on #4, mostly personal.

Here's Jerry's map:

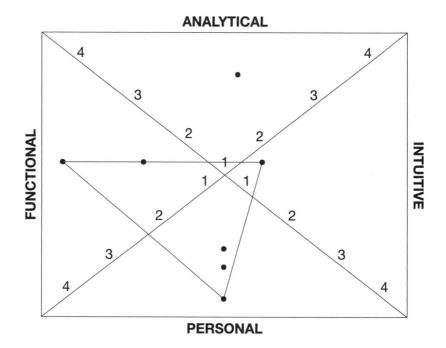

"Jerry, does this PSI map accurately depict your usual approach to solving problems?" I asked. "You nailed me," he laughed. "I'd have to agree that I'm keyed into relationships and a need to get control. Right?"

"Right," I replied. "The PSI results suggest you emphasize your need to understand where things are going in very functional and concrete ways. And, that often involves understanding and controlling how others you consider important are going to affect that control. Given the current situation at Kotak and Heims, let me ask you a question. Do you know what others in the company are likely to do, given the present challenges facing the company?"

Jerry frowned. "No. No, I don't."

"How does that make you feel?" I asked.

"Very, very anxious. I've never felt that way before," he replied. "I've known some of these people for almost forty years. And, while we've gotten pretty big, I still know most of our people quite well. I've tried to stay connected, to understand what they need and how they think. I do know many are angry and scared, and that scares *me*."

"Let's accept those observations as fact, and use them as a starting place for Sonja's development. But another question, Jerry: When you look at your PSI map, do you see anything missing or undervalued in your approach to solving your company's problems?"

"Analytical?"

"Bingo!" I said. "Another question: Did this crisis seem to come on quickly? I mean, by themselves, did the deaths in the warehouse, and the conflicts between groups, prompt you to call me and Sonja? Or did it start occurring to you earlier?"

"Earlier, actually. For a long time I may have been in denial. But then Sam [the CFO] told me the union stewards had gotten hold of our last quarter's financials, which showed us losing our shirts. That had been building for a long time. It wasn't just a sudden drop. If I'd been more analytical, I may have nipped the problem in the bud."

Sonja was learning something valuable as she eavesdropped on this "coaching" session with her own father. Both of them could see certain weaknesses in themselves, and they began to appreciate how much their respective strengths complemented each other.

More important than the particulars of a given problem is figuring out what you do know and don't know. As in a serious medical emergency, diagnosis will make or break the outcome. Neither Sonja nor Jerry possessed a complete picture. And, in Jerry's case, it was apparent that failure to balance his relationship control focus with the analytical had caused him to ignore the negative financial trends that fueled the anxiety and anger flowing from the warehouse incident and internal conflicts. The good news was that Sonja's and Jerry's combined PSI suggested an immediate first course of action.

Action

Action proceeds from diagnosis. As we've seen in the case study so far, even though time is of the essence and the issues are urgent in nature, there must be a diagnosis before taking action. Even as action is taken, the diagnosis provides guidance for continuous course correction. In the case of Jerry and Sonja, the first course of action was to refine and expand the diagnosis.

The PSI maps provided immediate guidance on the first action step required. PSI results convinced Jerry and Sonja that they needed to acquire more information before Sonja started developing solutions. Given the fact that people in the company were accustomed to Jerry's emphasis on relationships, Sonja needed to acquire her own information about how stakeholders viewed the organization. In addition to employees, she should especially explore relationships with customers, who had certainly been affected by the turmoil. The solutions for reconnecting and focusing their company would arise from the connection of seemingly disparate bits of information gleaned analytically, functionally, intuitively, and personally.

Finally, I could recommend an immediate course of action. Sonja would flesh out the facts while immersing herself in the company's culture. With Jerry taking the lead, the two would set up get-acquainted meetings with staff in the warehouses, sales and marketing, and with the drivers. After those sessions, Sonja would schedule individual meetings with people at all levels, asking such important questions as, "How can we improve? How can we better serve all of our stakeholders? How can we take control of our future and work more closely together as a family?"

The questions, though rather open-ended, would at least get the ball rolling in the right direction. While she recognized the power of the union's influence, rather than singling out individual stewards and representatives for one-on-one meetings, she targeted her effort on the company as a whole. She was dedicated to everyone's welfare, not specific concerns of special-interest groups.

I suggested that Sonja start with warehouse staff, move to sales and marketing, and then conclude with, and emphasize, the drivers. Most important, she should engage with everyone on their own turf, helping pack boxes in the warehouse, visiting customers with sales reps, and riding with drivers on delivery runs. What better way to gather the relationship-oriented information she needed? With such frontline engagement she would automatically gain personal and intuitive insight.

I should pause here to emphasize a key point. Whether or not you use the PSI map as a coaching tool, you should note that good coaches don't just tell a person to "go figure it out." Rather, good coaches directly engage in the learning assignments, particularly in the early stages of coaching. Coaching undertaken as an abstract exercise disconnected from the real world of work courts failure. Engagement courts success. Accordingly, Sonja not only immersed herself in the effort, she welcomed me to tag along for a little unobtrusive observation.

Identify the One Big Thing

Over the years I've distilled coaching into a few simple protocols. The most crucial? Identifying the One Big Thing (OBT). What one decision, what one action, will do more than anything else to get desired results? In Sonja's case, what OBT summed up the situation and established a clear point of departure for launching a plan for intervention and change?

After a week of immersion, I asked Sonja and Jerry to join me for a debriefing. First, I asked Sonja to define the OBT. She responded by fishing from her briefcase three yellow pads full of notes chronicling her adventures. She documented everything from confusing sales forms to error-prone warehousing systems to lack of toilet paper in the visitors' washrooms.

I let Sonja continue unabated for a good five minutes before I asked, "Can you cut through all these issues to the most important one? By the way, the information you've just shared with Jerry and me has been mostly analytical and functional, no? I'd like you to sit back and, not consulting your notes, tell us what you *feel* was the most insightful piece of information you picked up from all your meetings and, especially, from your travels with the drivers."

"Well," she replied, "while I picked up some anger, most people seemed really eager to make things work out. They deeply believe in the company, though they're worried sick about job security."

"That's interesting," I responded, "but is that the *single* most insightful information you picked up? Is that the One Big Thing that explains everything?"

Sonja paused before citing other observations, from the interests of the union stewards, to the ideas of sales and marketing people for higher incentives. Finally, after I repeated my questions so often it began to sound like a mantra, as I heard more and more a constant flow of analytical and functional information with an occasional personal or intuitive tidbit thrown in, Sonja exclaimed, "Oh, you mean the ketchup incident. Yes, that's it. It's all about the ketchup. That's the key to the whole mess. It ties everything together. Why didn't I see it before now? Straighten out the ketchup problem, and everything will come together."

The "ketchup problem" referred to an incident that Sonja had found out about when she had been riding with the drivers while they made deliveries to clients. On one of her visits with the owner of a first-rank, upscale "linen tablecloth" restaurant, Sonja got an earful. "Why can't you people deliver what you promise?" shouted the irate customer. "I asked for, and your salespeople promised, Heinz Ketchup. Yet, here again, I'm getting some no-name stuff. This is the last warning. If it happens again, Kotak and Heims is out, finished, kaput!"

Similar tirades about other wrong deliveries at two other stops confirmed in Sonja's mind a systemic performance problem, not a fluke or a "special variation," as quality gurus call it. Discussion with her drivers confirmed her suspicion.

"We're constantly taking the heat for this sort of screwup," proclaimed Jason, a driver for more than fifteen years. "If it's not ketchup, it's paper towels or oven cleaner. Sure, it's bound to happen now and then. But, the last year or so, it's the rule rather than the exception."

"It really gets down to lying to the customer," Jason continued. "Sales promises one thing, the warehouse packs another, and both point the finger at the other. By the time we get to the customer, we're set up for a fall."

At its highest level, leadership requires the ability to arrive at the intuitive insight necessary to link everything together. Such an insight unites the values and vision of the organization with the functional and analytical dimensions of operations in a way that resonates with the individual stakeholder; most especially, in this case, with employees.

The ketchup incident provided Sonja with such an insight. It gave her the platform needed to launch what became an extraordinarily simple, yet creative, process of organizational transformation and realignment.

The Breakthrough Insight

Achievers hunt for the One Big Thing that will give them both a focus and vehicle for the sort of achievement that propels them, their team, and their organization to the next level of performance. Remember, if coaching does not pursue an explicit performance improvement purpose, it can end up doing more harm than good. The OBT usually results from trying to expand problem-solving approaches and fill in the information map. Had we propelled Sonja into the operational battle before she had collected a

69

sufficiently complete array of information, we would have put the whole organization at an irresponsible level of risk.

With this diagnostic refinement in hand, Sonja could forge a strategy for taking the next level of action. Using the drivers as "customer reporters," Sonja assembled small cross-functional teams from across the organization to develop a situational analysis of where the company was and where it needed to be heading. Initially, she led the sessions personally. As they progressed, however, she turned them over to managers who had demonstrated a particular skill with the process.

The answers to these key questions were compiled and produced a situational analysis, which Sonja then shared in town hall meetings and through an internal corporate newsletter. There she announced the formation of problem-solving teams made up of and led by TalentLeaders selected from across the organization. The teams used the Team Problem-Solving System (TPS) presented in Chapter 8. The TPS was developed through the Talent IQ research and provided an efficient and consistent methodology for addressing important issues in a rapid but coordinated manner.

Sonja reported on problem-solving progress on a biweekly basis and prepared a special report on the company's turnaround in which she introduced herself, her mission, and the comprehensive steps under way to rededicate the corporation to the level of service that had given Kotak and Heims its special place in the market.

Our vigorous intervention soon began to produce results, and with them, the need for evaluation.

Evaluation

Evaluation must be an ongoing part of every coaching process. The method used must be consistent so that change in relation to the starting base line can be measured. While supplemental assessments can be incorporated along the way for highly focused learning purposes, use of the assessment system you started with at key milestones is the methodology of choice.

In Sonja's and Jerry's case, the reality profile of the corporation began to change for the better within three months and continued to do so at six-, twelve-, eighteen- and twenty-four-month milestones. Kotak and Heims not only returned to profitability, but did so at near-record industry levels. Customer and employee surveys, adapted from the Mission Assessment discussed in Chapter 6, revealed marked improvement in satisfaction, responsibility, and achievement.

Rates of turnover dropped and contract negotiations with unions were completed with unusually high levels of cooperation. Special achievements in the use of underutilized information technology investments led to a breakthrough in real-time, organization-wide communication.

For Sonja and Jerry, continuous monitoring of a problem-solving maturity through the PSI revealed steady and, in Sonja's case, dramatic progress. Two years later, Sonja led a merger of the company with a national distributor. Three years later, Sonja became the conglomerate's COO and president. Most important from Jerry's perspective, five years into the merger, fully 85 percent of Kotak and Heim's original work force remained happily employed.

Before undertaking any coaching, make sure, as we did with Sonja, that the person who tackles the problem can and will improve, which is the subject of our next chapter.

CHAPTER 4

Improve or Remove Talent-on-the-Bubble

TALENT CAN MAKE or break an organization. While talent aligned to achieve can move an organization to greatness, talent-on-the-bubble can take it down. This may seem painfully obvious, but many organizations pay little attention to confronting problematic behavior, thus failing to address one of the most important decisions organizations make: to improve or remove talent-on-the-bubble. When you ignore the problem and do not communicate with the person on-the-bubble, the behavior puts everyone at risk.

Our Talent IQ research found that effective leaders address on-the-bubble behavior decisively. TalentLeaders intervene early, leading people on-the-bubble through a candid examination of their present behavior, its possible progression, and its consequences. By doing so, high Talent IQ leaders were three times as likely to turn around on-the-bubble behavior as were other organizations. Not surprisingly, the overall commitment of employees reporting to such leaders ran nearly 50 percent higher than it was to average leaders; a result, as we will see, of the leader's taking responsibility.

Defining Talent-on-the-Bubble

What, exactly, is on-the-bubble behavior? It is any behavior that can compromise the achievement of an organization's mission. It undermines the ability of others to concentrate on that mission and achieve results for all stakeholders, from customers and the general public to shareholders and employees. Ignored, on-the-bubble behavior will metastasize like a malignant tumor, destroying all the healthy tissue around it. While it may start with an individual, it can expand to consume others until it grows so large it drags down individuals, teams, and the whole organization.

On-the-bubble behavior comes in various shapes and sizes. However, through the Talent IQ research, we have been able to distill it into fifteen types, as displayed in the Talent-on-the-Bubble Grid. These fifteen underperformers turn the three paths of achievement upside down, paving a downhill road to irresponsibility. As the behavior becomes more severely dysfunctional, it threatens achievement, partnership, commitment, optimism, and responsibility along the paths of service, innovation, and management. Let's examine the downward steps of on-the-bubble behavior for each of these paths and the corresponding traits each produces.

Talent-on-the-Bubble Grid

	Service	Innovation	Management
Fence-Sitting	Procrastinator	Narcissist	Stonewaller
Avoidance	Martyr	Deer in Headlights	Curmudgeon
Hostility	Gossip and Critic	Black Hole	Bully
Contempt	Manipulator	Fetalist	Bomber
Irresponsibility	Backstabber	Suicide	Predator

On-the-bubble behavior progresses from fence-sitting, which is characterized by a hesitancy to invest energy in moving out of the status quo. Fence-sitting produces procrastination, stonewalling, and increased self-absorption. If you permit this behavior to continue, it will descend into full-blown avoidance, where it takes the form of the self-justifying behavior of the Martyr and the Curmudgeon, or the depression and paralysis of the Deer in the Headlights. As avoidance becomes more extreme, it degenerates into hostility. For those following the service and management paths, it tends to express itself outwardly as gossip or bullying. When hostility turns more intensely destructive, it expresses itself outwardly through manipulation and the destructive outbursts of the Bomber, or inwardly through further retreat into self-destruction. Ultimately, on-the-bubble behavior will express itself overtly in backstabbing or predatory behavior, or inwardly as the employee continues to "blow it," essentially committing professional suicide.

Each of the paths progresses downward in a logical and predictable pattern, though a person on-the-bubble can, often and unpredictably, express traits from other paths as well. For example, talented people who primarily have manifested behind-the-scenes manipulative behavior can suddenly become more overtly predatory. However, since each of us usually employs one path as our core strategy for achievement, we usually find the negative traits of that path most troublesome. Let's examine each path to understand how this can happen.

The Path of the Backstabber

Descent into the realms of the Backstabber reveals the destructive power of affiliation run amok. It typically begins subtly as an act of mild avoidance or fence-sitting as someone withholds his or her usually cooperative response to calls for assistance and adopts a somewhat judgmental wait-and-see posture. This signals mild discontent, with the on-the-bubble person procrastinating on specific work assignments or personal requests. As procrastination leads to questioning by others, full-blown avoidance begins to emerge in the form of martyr-like behavior that projects responsibility and guilt for an individual's poor performance onto others. For

75

example, you'll hear the Martyr ask, "How do you expect me to fix the cyclotron when no one will answer my questions or provide the information I need?" The Martyr inaugurates a pattern of accusing others before he or she gets accused, usually with the result that others, trying to act responsibly, start to question their own, rather than the Martyr's, behavior.

Martyr behavior usually leads to overt hostility in the form of gossip and criticism, the first overt step toward ostracizing others. This is a dangerous development in which "removal" rather than "improvement" becomes the more likely choice of action. Social shunning deflects attention away from one's own limitations and toward another's. Expressed as a generalized attack on the inadequacies of the organization or others, it resorts to gossip and innuendo.

Gossip almost inevitably leads to overt manipulation, in which one person acts against another for the explicit purpose of inflicting harm. The Gossip invents and distorts information to suit his or her own agenda for survival, using the information as a means of manipulating others to ostracize and destroy others. As the manipulation takes hold, it undermines the core values, mission, and performance of the organization. Such manipulation, based on lies and distortions, is an act of cowardice. Here, the veil of deceit deflects accountability away from the deceiver and onto others, portraying them as offenders. This culminates in the ultimate act of destruction and betrayal: backstabbing.

The Path of the Predator

Predators are classic power players, and their behavior and their path to irresponsibility is painfully obvious. The progression from stonewalling to predation occurs quite rapidly, keeping the person one step ahead of improvement or removal. Where the Backstabber hides behind social shunning and manipulation, the Predator calculates a more direct route to power. That route begins with an obstructionist attitude that challenges other people's legitimate need for information or support. This behavior devolves into the expressive Curmudgeon, who makes sure "you pay for every encounter." The Curmudgeon's orneriness sometimes fools people into chalking it up to harmless eccentricity, when it actually masks burgeoning hostility.

Unchecked, the Curmudgeon plunges to the level of Bully very quickly. Where the schoolyard bully uses physical force, the organizational Bully uses verbal abuse, attacking people's character or the quality of their work or, if the Bully is their boss, threatening dismissal if they do not comply with his or her requests.

Inevitably, the Bully becomes a Bomber. Lacking the patience and cunning of the Manipulator, the Bully will explode in a direct and overwhelming public assault. "This is the last straw," explodes the Bomber. "You are destroying our organization and team with your disloyalty and selfishness. I, for one, want you out." The Bully designs "bombs" as personal and subjective assaults on an individual's self-confidence and trustworthiness. When the Bully, uncontested by bystanders, including superiors, progresses to the Bomber level, no one remains safe. Victims of the attack will be forced to leave or resign of their own accord.

Despite the havoc wreaked, the Bomber isn't finished. The first act of bombing merely tested the effectiveness of the technique. Like the schoolyard Bully-Bomber, a successful first episode leads to more attacks until a full-fledged Predator is born. The Bully usually selects as an initial target a weak opponent, one with relatively little support, experience, or knowledge. The Bully then bombs and waits to see the response. If none occurs, the Bully-Bomber selects the next victim. At first, the Bully relies on group indifference to succeed. But, as things progress, he or she relies on group anxiety and the fear that anyone might be next. In this way, the Bomber spreads distrust within the team or organization, leading inevitably to some backstabbing behavior as a member or members of the group begin to sell each other out to the Bully. Once the Bully progresses to full Predator status, he or she feels confident to

77

hunt and destroy at will. Beware of their behavior. It can result in an organizational catastrophe.

The Path of the Suicide

While both Backstabbers and Predators express their contempt and irresponsibility outwardly, the Suicide on-the-bubble employee directs energy inwardly, often with costly results. An exceptionally high percentage of Suicides come from the ranks of high-level knowledge workers, researchers, and innovators. Such people, by definition, have chosen to work in the world of ideas. As a result, they tend to rely on relatively small support groups. They relish problem-solving, be it analytical or intuitive. To the extent that servers and managers invest their self-worth in relationships, innovators invest their self-worth in abstract ideas. When threatened, they naturally turn inward.

The precipitating event that starts them on the downward path often involves some form of ridicule or attack by the Backstabber or Predator. It usually occurs as the result of some hiccup in the course of designing a new system, technology, or work process for which the innovator has been struggling to solve a particular problem. The Backstabber will likely spread gossip and imply that the innovator is out of touch with reality or is just not informed or creative enough. As the innovator receives word of the assertions, a sense of unease and inadequacy builds and can produce paranoia.

The Predator, by contrast, will see the struggling innovator as the weak member of the herd. Just as a lion will single out a weak or vulnerable antelope for attack, the Predator will pounce on a vulnerable member of the team during a team meeting in which the struggling innovator has admitted a shortcoming or a challenge with the project. The Predator launches a bombing run by saying, "You geeks think you're all smarter than everyone else. But you're not, and your mistakes, delays, and daydreaming are a huge waste of time, money, and energy. If you can't get it right, get out."

Innovators, by definition, challenge the status quo. They thus put themselves at higher risk of rejection and attack by those with strong territorial reasons for thwarting change. Unless you assess this special risk and afford protection and support to people developing new ideas, innovators will attract the attention of Predators and Backstabbers. You must stop backstabbing and predatory behavior as early along the paths as possible. Otherwise you'll pay a steep price, not in terms of the cost to the Backstabber or Predator, but in terms of the cost to the rest of the team and organization.

If you don't catch the behavior before the third level in the downward path, the Black Hole, removal becomes the only option. Rarely can you remedy the destructive effects of their behavior through coaching. The rehabilitative work will take too much time, money, and energy.

When injured, the innovator starts down the path toward self-destruction by assuming that the attacks, whether merited or not, signal a lack of support. His or her own behavior becomes increasingly narcissistic and self-absorbed, as the on-the-bubble innovator turns inward for both protection and healing. Note that most innovators don't wait around to suffer the full descent to the realms of Suicide. Possessing valuable transferable assets in the form of industry, scientific, or service knowledge, they can easily move to a competitor. That's one reason why on-the-bubble people from the service and management paths often feel jealous of innovators. Smart managers, therefore, pay special attention to protecting innovators from Backstabbers and Predators. If you don't, you risk creating a severe knowledge and skills deficit in your organization.

When others witness the self-destruction of an innovator, they fear for their own safety. Why, they wonder, has organizational leadership either initiated the events that caused such behavior, or stood callously and indifferently aside and allowed it to happen?

Either way, this talented group says to themselves, "Time to escape this harsh environment." Voilà! Talent exits stage right.

Be alert. What initially appears as offensive arrogance and self-absorption can mask the insecurity. Talented but insecure people often erect walls of vanity and self-indulgence to keep an intrusive and threatening world at bay. As narcissism takes root, Deer in the Headlights behavior (performance paralysis) emerges, signaling an avoidance of risks, including those associated with innovation. This nonresponsiveness takes a marked turn for the worse as it deteriorates to the level of the Black Hole, where no amount of input or outreach elicits a response. No matter how much information or attention goes in, nothing comes out. Whenever this behavior appears, you must seek serious professional intervention, and quickly, because the next step down the path, the Fetalist, presages some form of self-destruction.

The Fetalist on-the-bubble employee curls up into a self-protective inert ball. Whereas a person at the Black Hole stage might make the occasional foray out into the work world, the Fetalist hides from all interaction. And, when the Suicide occurs, usually in the form of a written resignation or in the de facto resignation of extended absence, you and the team may not have seen it coming because you hadn't even thought about or heard from the person in some time.

Before we leave the Suicide path, I must offer a sobering thought. The path to the Suicide produces a high percentage of those employees who become violent in the workplace. Sometimes, the Suicide, at a point of complete despair, adopts the traits of the Predator or Backstabber, taking violent action against those he perceives may have wronged him.

The Fifteen Talent-on-the-Bubble Types

Here's a summary of the most common traits of the types of employees described by the Talent-on-the-Bubble Grid.

SERVER

Fulfills basic human needs for physical connection, reciprocity, and relevance to daily survival needs for partners, both internal and external, in contrast with the following:

Procrastinator: a fence sitter; dislikes investing his or her energy; avoids commitment.

Martyr: an avoider; accusatory; self-righteous; blames others for his or her inadequacies.

Gossip: hostile; critical of others; spreads lies; intends to harm others.

Manipulator: contemptuous; deceives others by inventing/distorting information; convinces others to shun those he or she wishes to harm.

Backstabber: irresponsible; fakes relationships and deceives others to set them up for a severely slanderous and fatal surprise attack.

INNOVATOR

Fulfills the needs for continuous adaptation, change, and intellectual growth of the organization, in contrast with the following:

Narcissist: a fence sitter; outwardly arrogant and self-absorbed, while inwardly insecure and anxious.

Deer in the Headlights: an avoider who appears to be in a state of paralysis or shock; unresponsive, and unwilling and unable to engage others or respond to requests.

Black Hole: hostile; unresponsive; territorial and unproductive.

Fetalist: inwardly contemptuous; severely withdrawn; displays a zombielike demeanor.

Suicide: irresponsible and self-destructive; often resigns from his or her position either formally or by failing to show up; may express repressed anger by adopting the traits of the Predator or Backstabber.

MANAGER

Fulfills needs for security and community, securing alignment and distribution of resources—both human and material; provides direction regarding the rules and mores, goals, and objectives that guide the organization, in contrast with the following:

Stonewaller: a fence sitter; an obstructionist; challenges the legitimacy or need of another party for information or support.

Curmudgeon: an avoider; makes others "pay for every encounter."

Bully: hostile; attacks someone's character or the quality of their work; threatens employees with dismissal or a similar fate if they do not comply with his or her demands.

Bomber: contemptuous; destroys others' self-confidence; publicly assaults others; undermines others' value in the eyes of the team.

Predator: irresponsible; feeds off of others' insecurities; uses or destroys others to increase personal power; feels confident that he or she can hunt and destroy at will.

Regardless of its particular shape or size, undiagnosed and untreated on-the-bubble behavior will grow more and more destructive. To help you diagnose that behavior before it wreaks havoc, we'll use the Talent-on-the-Bubble Grid to examine real cases and show you how to implement make-or-break "improve or remove" decisions. One of my most memorable cases involves Cowboy Cal. I've changed names to protect the innocent and the guilty.

Case Study: Cowboy Cal

"Hey, Bobby Ray. Got some tabacca?" Cal yelled as he entered the ballroom and strode to the podium. "Sure do, Cal. Here ya go," replied the blindly obedient Bobby Ray from the back of the room as he threw a pouch of chewing tobacco over the heads of more than 300 hospital CEOs, medical staff presidents, board members, and other assembled officers of the fifty-plus-member hospital health-care system, Omnicare. Cal was Omnicare's chairman and CEO. The meeting had convened a few hours earlier to deal with important issues of patient care and profitability. Could Omnicare offer exemplary care and still increase profitability? Although Cal was not scheduled to address the convocation before lunch, he had decided to intervene and make sure, as he put it, "that everybody was saddled up on the right horses."

I can still see him resplendent in his custom-made Armani suit, $5,000 hand-sewn snakeskin cowboy boots, and gleaming white Stetson. A Choate and Dartmouth alum and a former assistant secretary at the U.S. Department of Commerce, he affected a Wild West demeanor. What Omnicare needed most, he insisted, was a John Wayne "take the bull by the horns" mentality. "If everybody just pulls up their chaps and gets on with it," he'd say, "everything else will take care of itself."

He wasn't about to let this panel and the audience "wimp out." After hijacking the podium he forcefully lectured the audience on the need for courage—cowboy courage—and the willingness to put profits, earnings per share, and stock options at the top of the company's priority list. When one hospital CEO interrupted to ask about the alarming rise in patient complaints and an increase in operating room safety problems, Cal yelled, "COURAGE, DAMN IT! C-O-U-R-A-G-E! Pull those chaps up, go forward!" With that, he exited the ballroom to the hootin' and hollerin' of his few loyal cowboy disciples.

Observing the spectacle as a consultant hired by the board, I would have laughed, had the issues not been a genuine matter of life or death. The vice chair of the board and designated representative of a majority of stockholders, Claire, had asked me to attend the conference and meet with the board regarding what she termed "a clear and present danger." To prepare for the engagement, I'd spent several weeks reviewing clinical and financial data, meeting with Cal, board members, executives, physicians, nurses,

83

other employees and, most important patients. Omnicare, I concluded, was teetering on the brink of catastrophe. And Cal was
unwittingly pushing it over the cliff.

Improve or Remove

The basic question facing Omnicare's board was the one every
leader grapples with when addressing talent-on-the-bubble:
improve or remove it. The organization simply could not risk the
alternative: let the situation continue and suffer the consequences.
Despite his cowboy affectation, Cal was smart, ambitious, and creative. Talent had gotten him his current job. However, his behavior was creating tension, confusion, and loss of mission focus at a
time when Omnicare could least afford it. Several cases of alleged
clinical neglect in key hospitals had led to severe criticism in the
media. Failure to respond appropriately, both externally and internally, did nothing but fuel plummeting confidence among patients
who worried about their recovery, employees who fretted about
their jobs, and physicians who feared malpractice suits. A resulting
reduction in admissions and reimbursement was setting the stage
for a financial meltdown.

The central question became: Could Cal provide the requisite leadership? Could he improve? Or, should he be removed? The
board needed an answer. Now!

The Talent-on-the-Bubble Process

With this preparation in hand, I invited Cal to an early-morning
meeting. Claire, who was the most powerful member of the board,
had introduced us, telling Cal in no uncertain terms that a majority
of board members disapproved of the corporation's downward spiral
and wanted Cal to meet with me to review how he viewed his role
and how he thought Omnicare should respond to the challenges.

Though Cal, like most people in a similar situation, did not realize the extent to which he had put himself on-the-bubble, he did respect Claire. She had put together the investment package that had propelled Omnicare's growth and enjoyed the confidence of other board members and the banks.

Why do so few people realize they're on-the-bubble? Denial explains some of it, but almost always they see little reason to fear the consequence of their behavior. IBM's Don Walsh refers to this as "complicity in blackmail." Others tolerate such behavior until it does real harm. In many cases, too, the organization does not set clear cultural mores and standards to govern professional behavior.

Bear in mind that the review process you're about to witness applies to *all* talent-on-the-bubble, not just senior executives. I've chosen Cal's case only because it so aptly illustrates the process. The more complex the position and the issues, the simpler you must make the review. Remember, complexity added to complexity equals chaos.

The on-the-bubble review protocol involves two basic steps.

First, establish a full context for understanding that the behavior exists. This includes all pertinent background. Only then can you embark on the sort of in-depth selection interview introduced in Chapter 2. You're looking to expose "make-or-break" alignment and "goodness of fit" issues. Our TalentLeader Study showed that in 55 percent of the cases, an organization could have anticipated and reduced the harmful effects of on-the-bubble behavior with a rigorous reselection interview.

Second, conduct the discussion using the Achievement in Action Grid (Introduction) and the Talent-on-the-Bubble Grid to analyze present behavior.

Cal's Work History

The review revealed a history of privilege. Cal had never held a significant job until after law school, when he assumed an associate's role in a large Dallas firm that had been serving family interests for two generations. He quickly became involved in politics, his true passion. Starting with an appointment to the state comptroller's office, he progressed to a junior position in the U.S. Department of Commerce, where, as he describes it, "I launched a networking campaign to end all networking campaigns. It really is about who, not what, you know. I was determined to make those good connections." Well, he did make them, networking his way to assistant secretary, a launching pad for what culminated in a career as a figurehead CEO for the banks and investors.

It was evident that Cal, despite his intelligence, education, and connections, lacked the requisite experience. But, as several Omnicare board members mentioned during discussions of Cal's fate, nobody had the courage to tell Cal to simply sport his Armani suits and smile at ribbon-cutting ceremonies—while letting the president and COO run things. Unfortunately, the COO, a seasoned veteran of the executive health-care wars, had been taken out of the picture five months earlier by a career-ending stroke. To the board's consternation, Cal had galloped into the vacuum, "put on his chaps," and assumed the COO's responsibilities in addition to his own.

As we reviewed Cal's work-life history, I asked him if he saw any deficits. He responded, "They told me when they recruited me two years ago that what they needed was someone to provide energy and vision for the future. My job was to inspire our investors and other stakeholders with the vision of how to do business in today's world. And, I think that's what I'm doing, what's needed, and what I'm good at. I think I see things the average leader in our company can't or won't see. And, why should they? They haven't had the preparation I've had."

I stopped him there. "Given that future, however, do you see any particular present challenges that may require skills you don't possess?" "Nope," Cal responded. "Oh, yeah, I don't know the details of some of the money stuff or the soap-opera problems of some of our physicians and patients, but that's why we have accountants, lawyers, and PR staff. My job is to keep everybody moving toward the future, not let us get dragged down in the mud of these pretty minor problems."

"How well equipped are Omnicare's leaders and your board to move toward that future?"

"Well, truthfully, we need to clean out the barn. We have too many naysayers around. They're the ones who interrupt the mission. Yes, we've got some issues, but we'll blow through them. I have to be real careful not to let other people's deficiencies take me down. That's why we shoot turkeys, not eagles."

On-the-Bubble Review

Did you see any evidence of the seven characteristics of achievement in Cal's background and excerpts of his interview? On a scale of 1 to 10, how would you rate him in terms of partnership, commitment, hope, responsibility, and humility? Despite his high mental IQ, he had the Talent IQ of a moron. Problem-solving? Forget it. In fact, his presentation at the conference epitomized problem *avoidance* and a failure to accept personal responsibility for the operational challenges facing Omnicare and its stakeholders. Cal operated as a lone ranger, committed only to his own limited and vague vision.

I wish I could say that Cal's story is the exception, rather than the rule. James Fallows, national correspondent for the *Atlantic Monthly* and author of *More Like Us*, a study of America's increasing loss of achievement ethic, points out that the greatest threat to pluralistic society is the increasing number of professionals and people of privilege who act like eighteenth-century aristocrats. They think their degrees, pedigree, licensure, and status entitle them to influence and prosperity, that they enjoy special rights that separate them from the "lower classes" who must earn their place in society through a day-to-day struggle. Instead of using their advantage as a launching pad for significant achievement and contribution, the aristocrats rely on them as entitlements that guarantee their position.

Of course, just because a manager or employee has come from wealth or advantages doesn't necessarily ensure that they'll fail as a leader. Many effective leaders—FDR and JFK come to mind—enjoyed privileged lives. However, if the aristocrats have not secured the work experience needed to understand the meaning of achievement and responsibility, their chances diminish dramatically.

Of the most talented leaders unveiled by our original Leadership IQ research, only 6 percent came from privileged backgrounds. The 6 percent succeeded *despite* their substantial and privileged family and educational credentials. They relied on the help of coaches and mentors to recognize their work achievement deficits and find ways to overcome them, often beginning work in the frontlines and earning their way up through the ranks. Their mentors saw to it that they received the kind of coaching and feedback that bestowed the "strategic humility" their upbringing never taught. This coaching and feedback canceled out the "silver spoon factor." Interestingly, not one of the benchmark leaders in the Leadership IQ study lacked up-from-the-ranks experience.

Cal was a classic aristocrat. Or to put it another way, he was a classic affiliator morphing into a predatory power player. This often happens to people who have climbed to the top of the social—not the skill—ladder, where no higher-up can guide them. Alone and without experience, they usually latch on to the most expedient model of behavior available—that of blowhard Bully.

Cal got ahead through networking. He believed his background differentiated him from others, to the point where he saw "cleaning out the barn" as the answer. His arrogance gave him a false sense of invulnerability. Thus he acted with impunity.

On a very practical level, Cal's interview underscored that he was not a "good fit" for either the CEO or COO role. In particular, he lacked both the work achievement history and professional insight needed to understand and deal with serious, even life-threatening issues. The company was facing a combination of interacting clinical, legal, public relations, and financial issues that threatened not just Omnicare's future but the lives of patients. Cal simply did not get it—and the board could no longer sit around waiting for him to get it.

Talent-on-the-Bubble Grid

To assist the Omnicare board, our consulting team utilized both the Achievement in Action Grid and the Talent-on-the-Bubble Grid. First, I asked the board to define the characteristics they required of their CEO. Discussion quickly led to the profile of an achiever. Then I asked, "Drawing on your knowledge of Cal's prior work history and present performance, does he match the profile of an achiever?" As we explored the characteristics displayed on the Achievement in Action Grid, I shared the results of my reselection interview with Cal, moving to a discussion of the Talent-on-the-Bubble Grid. This discussion helped to illustrate the implications of Cal's behavior over the past two years and at the conference.

Achievement in Action Grid

Paths of Action

	Service	Innovation	Management
Responsibility	Hero - Achiever	Hero - Achiever	Hero - Achiever
Optimism	Guide	Discoverer	Problem Solver
Commitment	Benefactor	Empowerer	Guardian
Partnership	Empathizer	Knowledge Leader	Builder
Achievement (pragmatism and humility)	Engager	Seeker	Organizer

The 7 Principles of Achievement

The board came to see Cal's behavior at the meeting as his routine operating style. Virtually every hospital CEO had been assaulted by it. Previously, however, the COO had cushioned Cal's bullying. Cal would pop into a key board, management, or medical staff meeting to deliver his "chaps" speech, criticizing those who lacked "courage," and leave without engaging in any discussion of pertinent issues. The COO would smooth ruffled feathers, but that did not stop many of Omnicare's leaders from flying the coop. Abuse talent, and it will leave. That's one reason "improve or remove" should preoccupy anyone trying to boost their Talent IQ.

Confront Arrogance and Impunity

Prior to the COO's stroke, few key people saw Cal's behavior as particularly threatening. But with the COO's cushioning effect no longer in place, they watched Cal's behavior deteriorate and started to worry about its impact on their careers. Free of any constraints and buoyed by the easy success of playing CEO cheerleader, Cal starting flexing his muscles.

More than 98 percent of the TalentLeaders in our study reported some variation of the Cal story. It's like the dirty secret in organizational life that no one wants to reveal. When someone like Cal displays on-the-bubble behavior and no one stops it, the Cals of the world take the lack of restraint as positive reinforcement for their actions. Not only do they continue their misbehavior, they actually intensify it in the sadly correct belief that they can act with impunity, without fear of interference or consequences.

If this strikes you as an exaggeration, just scan the *Wall Street Journal* for tales of misconduct by corporate executives, board members, bankers, consultants, and politicians at all levels. The consequences of such behavior will continue to plague us and our organizations until we end our own complicity in letting it go unchecked. That's where Omnicare's board stood: improve or remove, or suffer the consequences. The more we discussed Cal's behavior, the more it alarmed the board. Eventually, I called the question by asking the board members to summarize their views: "Considering what you know about Cal's past work history and present performance, do you see a good fit between Cal's talent and the company's needs now and in the future?"

The responses ran the gamut. One board member put it rather mildly: "We didn't think we needed an achiever when we hired him, we thought we needed a cheerleader. And that's what we got." Another got more critical, saying, "Yes, but we thought he had more self-awareness of his role and his limitations. He masked his arrogance so well." A senior member added, "He exhibited that 'cock-sure' selfish attitude from day one. For all the John Wayne silliness, there's no 'partner' in his vocabulary." Another joined in, "That includes us. He thinks he's beyond the boundaries of our authority. And that is our fault. We really didn't much care what he did as long as he left the serious management to the COO. Now, he's threatening our stability without any restraint on his personal egotism and personal ambition."

The conversation went on like that until Claire, the vice chair, bluntly said, "I for one feel immensely foolish and irresponsible. We forgot our fiduciary responsibility. This is a clinical health-care corporation, for God's sake. We should *never* have allowed ourselves to be seduced by the idea of a quick hit in the marketplace. While we now know Cal must be removed, we must take responsibility for his failure. We hired someone who will never be suited to the role."

To Improve or Remove?

Warren Brueggeman, former head of GE Nuclear Energy, liked to say, "You know when the decision is not to improve, but remove, when you no longer hold a positive expectation that an individual will make a contribution. It's intuitive but is backed up by a trail

91

of accumulated evidence and mishaps, some explained and some not, that tell you the risk of continuing is too great. It's all about the risk, first to your customers, then to your shareholders and associates, the ones who will bear the burden when all is said and done."

Claire had similarly summed up Omnicare's position with Cal: the risk was too great. Although Cal's behavior had not caused irreparable damage, it would, sooner rather than later. The decision to remove had virtually made itself.

Within days, the board appointed a pro-tem COO from within who would do the job while a search commenced for a CEO with significant achievement and proven commitment to quality patient care. The result? A restored reputation, confidence, a solid bottom line, and an increase in quality that saw several hospitals rise to the ranks of the industry's "Top 100."

Cal's leaving also sent the right message to others inside and outside the company: Omnicare valued achievers and would not tolerate persistent on-the-bubble behavior. Receiving the board's thanks and appropriate severance, Cal left Omnicare quietly.

Diagnosing On-the-Bubble Behavior

You'll recall that we used two tools, the Achievement in Action Grid and the Talent-on-the-Bubble Grid, to diagnose Cowboy Cal's behavior. These tools help us define poor behavior. Let's take a closer look at how it works, both conceptually and practically. The vertical axis on the Achievement in Action Grid marks the *ascent* toward responsibility; the horizontal axis displays the three paths of achievement.

Achievement in Action Grid

Paths of Action

		Service	Innovation	Management
The 7 Principles of Achievement	Responsibility	Hero - Achiever	Hero - Achiever	Hero - Achiever
	Optimism	Guide	Discoverer	Problem Solver
	Commitment	Benefactor	Empowerer	Guardian
	Partnership	Empathizer	Knowledge Leader	Builder
	Achievement (pragmatism and humility)	Engager	Seeker	Organizer

Talent-on-the-Bubble Grid

	Service	Innovation	Management
Fence-Sitting	Procrastinator	Narcissist	Stonewaller
Avoidance	Martyr	Deer in Headlights	Curmudgeon
Hostility	Gossip and Critic	Black Hole	Bully
Contempt	Manipulator	Fetalist	Bomber
Irresponsibility	Backstabber	Suicide	Predator

For every step toward responsibility on the Achievement in Action Grid, you find a corresponding step downward toward irresponsibility on the Talent-on-the-Bubble Grid, beginning with fence-sitting. Whereas achievers accept responsibility in advance as a routine matter, fence sitters hold back to see what options present themselves. This in turn prompts avoidance of who or what might threaten or challenge them. Avoidance leads to fear and hostility, culminating in acts of contempt. Left unchecked, this progressive behavior grows ever more destructive. Ultimately, it culminates in an act of irresponsibility that undermines the

93

well-being of all stakeholders, especially those most vulnerable and trusting: an organization's customers. For each path of achievement, the descent moves a person steadily into the dangerous worlds of the affiliator and the power player.

Let's apply the Talent-on-the-Bubble Grid to a few examples that will shed light on making improve-or-remove decisions.

The Case of the Deer in the Headlights

Jason was a rising star at IBM, and had worked hard to earn the chance to lead the launch of a critically important new product introduction in Japan. IBM had based its strategy on early success despite rather long odds, expecting that Jason could do it. Sadly, he failed—to the whopping tune of nearly $400 million in losses in one year alone. How did it happen, and what to do with Jason? These questions drove an investigation by a special crisis intervention team. In the end, the team concluded that somehow Jason could not bring himself to respond decisively to increasingly frequent and intense signals that the project was in jeopardy. He seemed paralyzed, like a Deer in the Headlights, frozen in his tracks despite the oncoming locomotive.

That's when our coaching team met him. Soon after the company brought him back stateside for a lengthy debriefing, his boss asked us to look into his possible reassignment elsewhere. "Why didn't you just remove Jason?" I asked his boss, a division president. "It's simple, really," he responded. "Jason is still a very talented person in whom we have now invested almost $50 million. And, he didn't fail alone. We all did. In fact, we left him out there at the point when we should have known he needed help. We loaded the expectations way beyond reasonable levels. Besides, we know he's an achiever; his past accomplishments speak for themselves. We still think he will make a significant return on that investment, especially if he can learn from this experience. That's why we want you to coach him as part of preparing a definitive report on why this Japanese venture failed. We hope he will turn this failure into a contribution that helps this corporation make more successful decisions in the future."

The Talent-on-the-Bubble Grid had isolated Jason's major problem: avoidance on the path of innovation. His work-life history showed just the opposite: he had always confronted challenges head-on. Also, his boss was right; many factors beyond Jason's control had conspired to immobilize him. We concluded that the right coaching could help him put this setback behind him.

The Case of the Backstabbing Bully

Job possessed a brilliant clinical mind. His academic medical and clinical credentials described a supremely talented engineer. "Why," he wondered, "doesn't everybody appreciate my superiority? Why must I suffer fools and incompetents?" Like the biblical Job, he chafed at the fact that the gods had punished him with undeserved torments. "I saved this place," he would whine to his confidants. He did deserve credit for impressive contributions to IntelliSound, a major manufacturer of acoustical devices. But there were others whose contributions were far more significant.

As head of the Acoustical Suppression Division, Job cultivated relationships with board members and other key players in the company. Given his value to the organization, many people tolerated his complaints and his penchant for gossip. He would flatter someone he saw as a potential benefactor, only to revile that person behind her back. His subordinates, whom he coerced into agreement lest he humiliate them in front of their peers or devastate them in their evaluation, kept their heads down and their mouths shut. Of course, he never fired anyone who bowed to his opinions, regardless of their performance. Bullies never want to give up obsequious and compliant soldiers who will do their bidding.

Unchecked, Job's behavior progressed classically through the hostility of the Critic to the contempt of the Manipulator. Peel away his veneer of arrogance, and what was there? Deep-seated insecurities plagued by self-doubt and a craving for approval and respect. He used criticism and gossip as knives. The insecure often try to cut others down to their own pathological size—a good definition of "backstabbing."

When IntelliSound's CEO finally tried to counsel Job about his backstabbing and bullying behavior, he only fueled Job's resentment and anger. Each time the CEO reached out, Job became more outwardly obsequious and more inwardly hostile, projecting his anger through increasingly vicious innuendo and sly professional criticism, often coercing his bullied subordinates to spread the word.

As many backstabbers do, Job stayed up late at night crafting an elaborate campaign pitting manager against manager, executive against executive, and, ultimately, board chair against the person who had hired him, the CEO. "How can a superficial charmer lead a major institution?" he slyly questioned. "Without me and, perhaps, some of my people, he could never survive."

Job was not stupid. He was clever. But his was dangerous cleverness because he worked in the shadows, trapping others in a complicity that prevented them from sharing their disapproval of Job's behavior with others and connecting the dots of his destructive actions.

What would you have done with Job? Could he improve? When the CEO finally connected the dots of gradually accumulating concerns of talented leaders who were thinking about leaving the company or were suffering from injuries inflicted by Job's hand, the CEO made the best decision for all concerned and summarily terminated Job.

Decision: Remove

The Case of the Manipulator

On-the-bubble behavior can affect any organization. Sarah was a rising star in the academic world. From Brown University, where she earned a doctorate at age twenty-five, she went to the *New York Times* and became part—albeit a small part—of a Pulitzer Prize–winning reporting team. From there she returned to the halls of academe as an associate professor at a good Midwestern university, where she quickly rose to associate dean. After a year she moved on to dean of a noted school of journalism, where she stayed for two years before becoming academic vice president and dean of a 15,000-student college at a branch of the State University of New York.

Sarah had a gift for storytelling. She loved to tell tales and, sometimes, included them in memos. Her career had moved at such a blinding speed that she had always stayed a step ahead of any consequences of her richly embellished stories. Without any negative feedback, she paid less and less attention to cold, hard facts. Consequently, after articulating her outrage over presidential decisions to alter her proposed budget, she was surprised when the president summarily dismissed her for what he called "irresponsible and insubordinate behavior." Flabbergasted, she retorted, "I am entitled to my rights of free speech. You're trampling on the First Amendment!"

The president replied, "I know the First Amendment very well, but I'm equally aware of my fiduciary responsibilities and your contractual obligations. Our responsibilities, yours and mine, include protecting this institution from vicious attacks and from efforts to undermine the established and honored governance process of the larger academic community. In both regards, you have failed to abide by the terms of your contract.

"In addition to this most recent memo, which makes strong, unwarranted, and unjustified accusations, you have written others, which allege shortcomings ranging from the personal to the criminal. Not only have you abrogated established protocol for dealing with such issues, but you have produced no material evidence to support any claims, distorting virtually every issue to the point where your recklessness has caused unpardonable personal and professional harm. That behavior is astonishingly irresponsible.

You're fired." Sarah behaved like the prototypical Suicide, one of the worst forms of on-the-bubble behavior because its degree of irresponsibility cannot easily or quickly be improved. The president could not have made a decision to improve.

Decision: Remove

Tough Calls

It's never easy to fire someone, even if you have developed an airtight case for removal. Emotions, yours and the other person's, always run high, and nothing clouds a confrontation more than feelings of anger and regret. However, taking action to address on-the-bubble behavior is one of the most critical Talent IQ skills. As our study revealed, this skill has become essential in today's rapid-fire and shrinking world. On-the-bubble behavior can infect an organization like a virulent and contagious illness that can bring progress to a grinding halt. Leaders cannot afford the risk of such a rapid and comprehensive contagion.

A few cautions. First, resist the "hypocrisy factor." Any tolerance of on-the-bubble behavior flies in the face of fundamental mission values, the drive to achievement, and partnership with the customer. Eventually, on-the-bubble behavior will hurt all stakeholders. You do no favors to stakeholders, or the person on-the-bubble, by letting it go unchecked, hoping that it will magically improve. It won't.

Second, as we discussed earlier in the book, keep the "magnet of achievement" in mind. It does more than anything else to propel the organization to success. Tolerated, on-the-bubble behavior strengthens the "anchor of negativity" that can plunge your organization to the bottom and drive off achievers.

Third, dealing with a person displaying on-the-bubble behavior by improving or removing him benefits him, too. I should know. It happened to me. Promoted to an associate academic dean's job, I started flexing my newfound muscles like a Bully. In charge of the instructional budget for the college, I proceeded to make harsh demands of my previous boss and department head. When I received a call from him inviting me to lunch, I expected him to congratulate me on the great job I was doing. Instead, he initiated the discussion by inquiring about family, friends, and some mutual interests. Before we ordered lunch, he looked me in the eye and said, very calmly: "Your recent actions? Stop it. You are a much better person than your present behavior suggests." That's all he needed to say. I felt ashamed and vowed to give my bullying muscles a rest. Of course, I thanked my mentor profusely, not just in words, but by taking this lesson to heart. I improved. Had I not, I would have wound up removed.

Throughout the Talent IQ research project, we heard hundreds of similar stories. Telling someone that he or she can improve is a sign of deep caring and an act of true responsibility. Achievement requires responsibility. Confrontations like mine and the others can go smoothly if you keep the Achievement in Action and Talent-on-the-Bubble grids handy. Will that make everything hassle-free in your organization? No. You will always encounter conflict when talented people are involved in an endeavor, which is the subject of the next chapter.

CHAPTER 5

Communicate Commitment

AT 4:00 A.M. IN WEST ISLIP, New York, ten miles from Kennedy Airport, the phone rings on the nightstand next to Bill Shaw's bed. Within seconds he is fully awake and snatches up the receiver. Bill heads up World Class Shipping, a major worldwide logistics company, and he still makes himself available 24/7.

"Hi, Dad, it's Billy," he hears through the static. "I'm in Qatar." Bill (Billy) Shaw III has followed in his father's and grandfather's footsteps. Bill Shaw Sr. retired as director of U.S. Customs at Kennedy Airport. Bill Jr. started World Class Shipping, where Bill III serves as vice president of development.

"What are you doing in Qatar? You're supposed to be in Baghdad," Bill asks his son.

"We were flagged off. They closed Baghdad because they were under fire. We came here 'cause we've got to go by land. I'm getting a truck convoy together. We'll be leaving in about an hour."

"A truck convoy? No way. You're going to get yourself killed. Stay right where you are until I call you back." Wide awake now, Bill phones another member of the World Class Shipping network in theater who quickly assembles an armored escort with U.S. Army helicopter gunship overflight. Within hours, Billy, encased in body armor and packed into an armored Humvee, arrives safely in Baghdad.

Effective communication at World Class Shipping means more than cell phones and e-mail. Every hour of every day, Bill and his team cut through noise and confusion to make sure that essential messages come through loud and clear. They realize they must communicate their commitment every day in every way possible.

As Bill Jr. himself observes, "Our service partners are spread all over the globe. They are our most important asset and they need to know they're never alone, that we will always be there for them, no matter what personal, operational, or customer challenge they face. But, this takes more than wanting to do the right thing; it takes a total commitment to timely and clear communication that makes commitment a reality."

Bill Shaw has insisted that World Class Shipping (WCS) make communication systems central to its core mission. As a result, his company has confronted what I call "people noise" head-on. By "people noise," I mean all those sounds and activities that tend to disrupt or even cancel out the clear communication that is essential to building and holding together the talented people necessary for success.

Given that WCS has the challenge of solving problems in locations as far-flung as Baghdad and Dubai, the company has developed the most advanced and responsive communication network in its industry, as recognized by its receipt of countless awards from the World Cargo Alliance, the largest logistics association in the world.

"Our strategic goal is to build a universal partnership of commitment," explains Chris Shaw, Bill's second son and the company's chief technology officer. "We want our associates and our customers to be able to communicate and support each other as if they were in the same room. But, we know we have a huge challenge dealing with all the people noise that threatens our communications every day. It would be bad enough if we were just trying to keep people connected here in New York City; however, we're trying to hold a worldwide community together. In our business, people noise could literally kill us."

People Noise: A Threat to Commitment

On the field of battle . . . the spoken word does not carry far enough. . . .
Gongs and drums, banners and flags, are means whereby the ears and eyes
of the host may be focused on one particular point.

—Sun-Tzu, *The Art of War*

Several years back, one of our foremost TalentLeaders, the late Dr.
Gerhard Koch, former consultant to NASA and professor emeritus
of chemical engineering at the State University of New York, shared
an insight with me. Over a memorable dinner with his son Stephen,
winner of the Turing Award in Computer Science (the Nobel of the
field), and Dr. Wilson Greatbatch, inventor of the pacemaker and
member of the Smithsonian's Hall of Inventors, we were chatting
about technology, human psychology, and connection.

"Emmett," Dr. Koch observed, "where the challenge for scientists is to answer the question of how to help make technology
work for the good of humankind, yours is to answer the question of
how to help keep people connected and manage the people noise
that could keep them apart. Engineers and physicists manage
noise in electronic systems. The same is true, I think, in everyday
interpersonal communications. After all, we humans are all just
large electronic cells projecting our signals to each other." That
comment lit a light bulb over my head. How true! Most of my life
I had been wrestling with the problem of people noise without
knowing what to call it.

Talented people, I realized, were especially prone to the effects
of people noise. Because they are so focused on achievement, the
interference, resistance, crosstalk, attenuation, and glitches that
could obstruct their ability to make progress would be especially
aggravating. By contrast, affiliators and power players might not
only welcome noise as a smokescreen for their real intentions, but
actually be the primary sources of noise itself. The importance of
managing and, if possible, eliminating noise became, I realized,
an imperative for clear communication and, most especially, for

103

sustaining the commitment that held all successful organizations together. Without the ability to manage noise and communicate commitment, it would be difficult, if not impossible, to retain talented staff and customers, as well as generate the revenue necessary for success.

With this new focus, I encouraged Bill Shaw to develop a people-noise management system so that customers in Mongolia or the Antarctic could feel as connected to the talented staff of World Class Shipping as did customers in Manhattan or Alabama.

The resulting system has enabled WCS to transport aid to Baghdad in wartime, to Bangkok after the tsunami, to Pakistan and Afghanistan after the major earthquake there, and to Sarajevo in the wake of upheaval. WCS delivered heart-lung equipment to Russia for Boris Yeltsin's heart surgery, and it will someday supply oxygen to a human colony on Mars, should humankind ever take that next giant step.

Bob Hong, CEO of Pacific Logistics and a fellow member of the World Cargo Alliance, says this about WCS: "Most people think that communicating and doing business on a global level requires chameleon-like communication. Bill Shaw Jr. has taught us all that it's virtually the opposite. He . . . speaks his mind, has the same standards and message for everyone he deals with. So, why are he and the company that mirrors his values so remarkably successful? I think it's simple: He is authentic, predictable, treats all people with the same respect, and lives up to every commitment. People trust him with their goods, their money and, sometimes, even with their lives, because he is the real definition of integrity. And, he projects this set of values through the most carefully designed communications outreach system in the industry."

Managing People Noise

Bill and other TalentLeaders have helped us design an eight-step approach to dealing with people noise.

8 *Steps to Clear Communication*

Step 1	Define the Challenge
Step 2	Diagnose the Cause
Step 3	Create a Plan
Step 4	Tune In
Step 5	Tune Out—or Take Out
Step 6	Cut Through
Step 7	Stay on Message
Step 8	Practice Rapid Response Communication

Now, let's look more closely at each of these steps and watch as Bill Shaw implements them at WCS.

Step 1: Define the Challenge

You can't meet any challenge without awareness of it. Too often, leaders skip this obvious step with the result that their stakeholders—the most talented among them—do not understand why a company has embarked on a particular course of action. Therefore, first and foremost, you want to define the specific problem that people noise is creating in your organization.

Bill Shaw succinctly defines the challenge to WCS:

"Large and rapid swings in the economic and political environment affect the global economy, creating a volatile and dangerous day-to-day work environment. Invasive messages of turmoil and struggle create a constant undercurrent of noise that can obscure what is happening at the local level. If WCS doesn't maintain connection at the local level through clear communication, our business will ultimately fail."

After Bill issued this statement to his associates throughout WCS's worldwide network, he invited everyone to work together to solve the problem. As he told me, "I wanted everyone to know we understood they faced a tremendous challenge, and I wanted to assure them we would get on top of it and that they would be central to the effort from the start. The results were amazing. Input flowed in and worldwide conferencing and problem-solving brought us closer than ever. The results? Exceptional growth in sales and profits."

Step 2: Diagnose the Cause

Scientists recognize five types of noise that can disrupt a signal: resistance, interference, attenuation, crosstalk, and glitches.

Resistance

Resistance is noise that distorts a signal as it travels through certain media. A copper wire will distort a signal less than will a steel wire. Just as the unique composition of the medium affects the transmission and reception of a signal, so does the unique composition of a group of people who are communicating with each other.

Each of us processes information differently. Those differences can lead to resistance noise. While ethnic, racial, gender, national, and socioeconomic differences affect the way people receive and transmit information, neurological research tells us that such differences fall into four basic categories, which we will discuss more fully later in this chapter: analytical, functional, intuitive, and personal (see also the discussion about problem-solving styles in Chapter 3). Each of these relationship styles determines individual communication preferences; when a person relying on one style doesn't tune in to another person's different style, the potential for miscommunication skyrockets. Because every organization includes people operating with all four styles, leaders must learn how to tune in to each type to get their messages across. In the next section, we'll discover how high-performing leaders reach their audience by crafting messages that meet diverse communication needs and expectations.

Interference

Interference represents an act of communication sabotage—someone deliberately trying to prevent your message from getting through. If resistance means "I just don't get it," then interference means "I don't *want* to get it." Examples include an office rival disrupting a meeting, people "forgetting" to pass along important information, and outright defiance.

Interference invariably stems from someone trying to wield power and control. People like to exercise some degree of control over their lives, and as life gets more unpredictable, confusing, and frightening, they try to restore some sort of order. Stakeholders committed to the organization try to assert control by helping the organization adapt to the changing environment. Those not committed to the organization will wield their power to promote their self-interest over the interests of the whole. In turbulent times, high-performing leaders remain alert for signs of interference, and either redirect the energy of interferers into more productive channels or, in extreme cases, remove them from the organization.

Attenuation

Attenuation weakens a message as it travels farther and farther. Engineers address this problem with electronic transformers and boosters along the line carrying the signal. Similarly, leaders must often "boost" signal strength to overcome the weakening effects of distance. If you've ever felt that your message disappears as it travels up or down through the corporate bureaucracy, then you understand how attenuation can ruin communication. Often, by the time information gets from leadership to frontline workers or vice versa, the original message has become a faint echo. While attenuation sometimes occurs as a result of geographical separation, it more often results from complexity. Imagine a tightly coiled ball of wire; while the two ends may lie only a few inches apart, the pathway between them may run dozens of feet. The pathway of communication in an organization sometimes works like that. Another department may be on the same floor as yours, but for purposes of communication it might as well be on Mars. High-performing leaders learn how to slice through organizational complexity and bring their messages directly to the people who need to hear them.

Crosstalk

Have you ever tried to concentrate when several people all vie for your attention at the same time? Scientists call this phenomenon crosstalk, a bunch of signals losing clarity as they clamor to be heard. Today's organizations often seem like one big shouting match. At any given moment, a leader's message must compete for attention with all the other conversations going on in the organization. To strengthen the signal strength of their message and prevent it from getting lost in the "background roar," high-performing leaders learn how to simplify, amplify, and clarify their messages.

Glitches

Glitches are unexpected disruptions that knock communications off track. Unlike the other four types of noise, with their definable causes, glitches seem to come out of the blue. No matter how well you craft a message, you can expect an unexpected glitch to distort it. I say "unexpected" only because you never know exactly when glitches will strike. Successful leaders prepare for glitches by developing the flexibility and resilience to respond adroitly when a crisis does hit.

In Bill Shaw's case, he grappled with all forms of people noise. Bill understood that noise could undermine the commitment he was trying to infuse into every part of the global partnership network. If noise dominated the environment, then the commitment and trust he had built with talented staff, customers, and new venture partners could be lost or diminished. The results could be high turnover of staff, and loss of clients, partners, and, ultimately, revenue. Bill understood that developing insight into each form of noise and how it could impact World Class Shipping was essential both to reducing current noise levels and preventing its emergence in the future.

Step 3: Create a Plan

Once you understand the five types of noise, you can take stock of your own, another person's, a team's, or an organization's communication problems, thus creating a "noise inventory" you can use as a basis for planning solutions. This makes it possible to create plans based on concrete evidence rather than on vague feelings and emotional assessments.

Bill Jr. and his WCS team took just such an inventory and discovered that all five types of noise affected their global organizations. Each WCS team member contributed evidence on which Bill could base his plans. "The first thing that hit me was attenuation," Bill recalls. "We know we're all spread out, but the potential for loss of connection was so high that we immediately threw a team together to address it.

"The conclusion was an unusual and highly personal use of the Internet coupled with 24/7 staffing by a member of senior management. No matter what day or time, in whatever part of the world, a senior executive of the company would be immediately available to address complex issues. We also brought our worldwide team together in one-on-one small team teleconferences no less than biweekly, with individual managers holding at least weekly solution-development meetings with subordinates. Then, at least three times a year, all worldwide regional leaders met at World Cargo Alliance meetings. This is supplemented by our frequent forays into the field, where we always spend time at our regional offices as well as with our clients. We know we have to boost our signal-to-noise ratio, and we are constantly refining our system."

Chris Shaw, the chief technology officer, offered his unique perspective: "It became strikingly clear that we had to tune in more effectively. We formed a team representing every contingent and key market area of the world and asked the question, 'How can we reach our customers and our associates where they live, not make them come to us?'"

After weighing numerous solutions to the problem, the WCS team chose a creative one. "We decided to build 'empathy bridges' over the Net, where we could meet the four basic information needs of particular regions, countries, and markets. We identified over a hundred distinct Web site locations we needed to construct. Now, someone in Mongolia can key into WCS Mongolia in their own language and find a connection that honors their uniqueness and needs while linking them to our worldwide support system. We used the 'relations style' matrix developed by the Talent IQ research project to help us find common denominators and make the project much more manageable than we ever thought possible."

Chris also tackled glitches. With some other WCS "Special Forces" people, he catches and responds to problems in the field that require immediate attention. "Since we've begun rigorously diagnosing, planning, and acting to reduce noise, the number of glitches has gone down dramatically. We are now catching problems as they emerge and before they blossom into full-grown crises."

Ellen Shaw, the company's treasurer, coped with interference and crosstalk. "The noise reduction process has helped reduce the noise at all levels of our operations, including collection of receivables. We now have very little crosstalk where we are thrown back and forth from one person to another, hearing different and conflicting messages. And, the number of 'interferers' is way down."

Step 4: Tune In

Contemporary neurological research shows that individuals tend to receive and process communications to fulfill one or all of the four information needs: intuitive, analytical, personal, and functional. You'll recall that these same categories appear in the Problem-Solving Inventory (PSI) Map in Chapter 3. They not only reflect our problem-solving styles; they also describe our information needs. Each of us tends to emphasize one of these needs in our communication style, although experience and training can help anyone extend their repertoire. We develop these styles through a complex mix of heredity, nurturing, and education that derives from a full range of ethnic, religious, national, and environmental factors.

Communication Needs/Styles Grid

You can use the following Communication Styles Grid the same way you used the PSI Map.

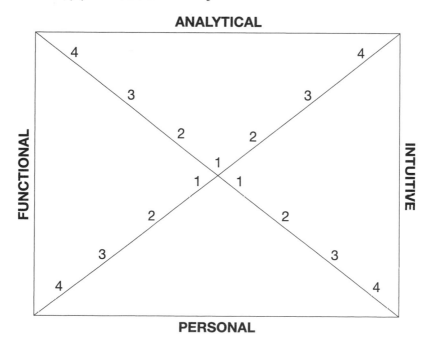

111

Analytical Communicators

Analytical communicators prefer structure, analysis, and hard data. They value facts, technical expertise, and systematic methods for solving problems and getting results. When communicating with them, you must effectively get your message through by basing it on data and logical arguments.

Functional Communicators

Functional communicators also prefer structure, but they want to know what to do with the data. They value planning, decisive action, and tangible and immediate results. You must deliver your message in a down-to-earth and practical way, yet you must answer the question, "How can we get the job done?"

Intuitive Communicators

Intuitive communicators are nonlinear and rational. They focus on the big picture or vision of the future, rather than the here-and-now. They place a high value on concepts, imagination, and creativity. When dealing with intuitive communicators, it's best to talk in terms of strategy and innovation.

Personal Communicators

Personal communicators combine nonlinear thinking with emotion. Dynamic, friendly, and charming, they value empathy, sensitivity, and the opportunity to work with others. When dealing with personal communicators, you should focus on the human side of an issue.

WCS, a global operation that deals with every race, creed, nationality, and communication style in the world, needed a communication system that took all four styles into account.

An effective message includes four subtle variations on the same message, striking a nerve in each style of communicator. We call this sort of communication "M-Pathic," which means the ability to empathize with all types of people and communicate along multiple paths. Chris Shaw and his team emphasized this very approach when developing their worldwide empathy bridges.

Reliance on just one style leads to ineffective communication. For example, if you give a "just the facts, ma'am" analytical presentation, everyone but analytical communicators will tune you out. The same holds true for a purely functional, purely intuitive, or purely personal message. If you take your analytical message and add a functional element (for example, "the data says that we should do X, Y, and Z this year, and Tina's team will take charge of that"), functional communicators will pay attention because the practical message grabbed their attention. Add a personal message (such as, "I understand that might make us uncomfortable . . .") and an intuitive message (for instance, "but it will help us serve our customers better, and become more innovative and thus ensure a more competitive position") and you have tuned in the entire audience.

Step 5: Tune Out—or Take Out

As we said earlier, interference amounts to nothing less than a guerrilla attack on a leader's attempts to communicate. You can usually recognize interference quite easily, even when it masquerades as simple misunderstanding or constructive criticism. The tip-off? You detect ill will from the other person, either veiled or blatant. In other words, if you think someone is conspiring against you, you're probably right.

All forms of interference arise from a dysfunctional and self-centered need to wield power and control. How someone expresses interference, however, depends on that person's idiosyncrasies and communication style. Analytical communicators tend to contradict your messages with data, while personal communicators may attempt to manipulate you emotionally to thwart the message. Functional communicators will resort to policies and procedures to block your communications, while intuitive communicators may dismiss them because they lack sufficient creativity or scope.

Try to sort out the motivation of potential interferers before they launch a full-blown attack on you. Interestingly, you can use one weapon to combat them all: *tune them out*. Whatever their style or agenda, if you let interferers block your communication, you will find your message disrupted and your plans compromised. Even when they can't stymie your efforts, interferers will steal valuable time and energy better spent serving your organization and its customers. Don't give the squeaky wheels any grease, and they'll stop rolling. If they don't, you may need to roll them toward the door; *remove them from your team, department, or organization immediately.*

Behavioral research supports this approach: ignoring inappropriate behavior tends to help the perpetrators extinguish it on their own. If they don't improve? You know the answer to that by now.

Use a three-part strategy for dealing with interferers. First, separate self from substance. React to an incidence of interference in a way that respects the person and his or her position, yet makes it perfectly clear that you will not accept the behavior because of its negative impact on the organization. Begin by saying, "I understand," and then affirm the person's concern. For example, if you encounter a functional communicator who resists a new initiative, you might say, "I understand your concern that we've never done things this way before, and that we haven't set up a procedure for this yet, but . . ." Or, in the case of a personal communicator who hopes to manipulate your emotions: "I understand that you worry about taking a personal risk here." Second, follow with an analytical and functional statement: "However, the results of our research indicate that we need to get the following done . . ." Third, conclude with a visionary statement that appeals to the intuitive: "And if we don't do this, we won't be able to fulfill our mission."

It's a useful mantra: "I understand; however; because."

I understand . . .
However . . .
Because . . .

What happens if the script doesn't work after a repetition or two? Try this line: "It appears that you do not understand my message. As a result, you're disrupting our goals. You and I will meet privately to talk about this issue. We simply cannot continue in this fashion." That private talk may well evolve into an exit interview.

Step 6: Cut Through

Wendell Province, CEO of Midas, Inc., cut through the noise by going directly to the frontlines of service. When Province took the helm in 1998, he found an organization mired in a strange quagmire, having opened company-owned muffler and brake shops in direct competition with shops owned by franchisees (even, in some cases, putting both a company-owned and a franchise store on the same street). Understandably, affected franchise own-ers had rebelled. Amidst the uproar, Province—who lives by the motto "Life isn't about contracts; it's about trust"—cut through the noise and turned Midas's culture on its head. As one of his first acts as CEO, Province met with individual shop owners to reaffirm his commitment to them. He then promptly sold off the company stores and sent each franchise a share of the profits.

115

Next, he promised every Midas franchise owner a discount on a different part each month, enabling them to boost sales by offering monthly specials. Finally, Province cemented his relationship with franchise owners by covering the cost of a national television ad campaign. In bypassing the ordinary chain of command, Province shunned isolation and complexity and forged relationships with the people who really drive his organization's success.

Step 7: Stay on Message

You must, of course, do more than just cut through the noise; you must do it with a clear and consistent message. An unclear or confusing message will get lost in all the crosstalk. That's why you must continually strengthen your message through consistency, repetition, clarification, and simplification.

We've seen how WCS stays on message with its global network, but what happens when leaders don't do it well? In 1990, Sears, at the tail end of a five-year slump, found itself bombarded with accusations of fraudulent business practices in its auto centers. All of this came at a time when the morale of the company's more than 300,000 employees had plummeted to an all-time low. To turn things around, CEO Arthur Martinez assembled the "Phoenix" team (as in the mythical bird that rose up from its own ashes), which launched a series of town hall meetings designed to inspire and energize employees. However, the company's efforts failed. According to Stephen Kearns, director of the project, "We dropped the ball on this one." The town hall meetings did draw people together, but they failed to convey a consistent message of participation-driven change. Although the executive team and the regional managers all received that message, the district managers, the ones who conducted meetings for store managers, did not. Six months into the project, participation fell to 30 percent. At the same time, Martinez's two top executives, who had never supported the initiative, began rigorous cost cutting without employee input, an act that diminished the goodwill that Sears had worked so hard to build. In both word and deed, Sears's executives undermined their company's turnaround by not sending a consistent message.

Step 8: Practice Rapid Response Communication

Glitches can strike without warning. In reality, certain conditions usually presage them. No company, not even a great one, can prevent them, though any company can anticipate and prepare for crises, no matter what form they take. Because crises invariably increase all forms of noise, you want to make sure that you have installed the most effective noise reduction system: rapid response communication. To do that, TalentLeaders rely on one battle-tested rule: *Remain open and compassionate.*

Glitches usually come in the form of financial, operational, legal, or public relations crises. Such crises can alarm the most talented people in the organization because they threaten achievement. Whatever the particular crisis, stakeholders will place some blame on leadership, usually with good reason. TalentLeaders quickly accept responsibility for any part they may have played in the crisis. They do not deny or hide the truth. Instead of focusing on how to protect themselves, they focus on protecting their talented people and their customers with compassion and honesty. And they do it *promptly.* They don't wait for the crisis to start driving talent away.

WCS runs into glitches every day, unexpected calamities such as the closure of the Baghdad airport related early in this chapter. Whatever the glitch—the escalation of a civil war in Africa, a terrorist bomb explosion in Singapore, a heart attack in the Kremlin—Bill Shaw and his team of talented people respond rapidly with their state-of-the-art network of empathic bridges. Problem-solving in their world (indeed in all companies these days) is a 24/7/365 proposition.

117

Communication Leads to Commitment

Managing noise in organizational life is essential to clearly communicating the commitment it takes to bond customers, employees, and venture partners and other stakeholders into a cohesive whole. Without that, you risk losing your most talented employees. The global communication challenge facing Bill Shaw and his team highlights the challenge every organization faces, whether it realizes it or not. While global enterprises are likely to face noise issues in ways that bring risks to light more immediately, every organization needs to heed the lessons from World Class Shipping if it is to be effective in retaining and developing the talented people it needs to provide excellence in service and the customers who believe commitment is the reason for seeking it.

CHAPTER 6

Measure Responsibility

THE FOUR-MINUTE MILE. A 7–4 victory in game seven of the World Series. A forty-foot putt to win the Masters by one stroke. Winner "by a nose" at the Kentucky Derby. No matter what the activity, no matter what the job, achievement depends on some form of measurement. Without measurement, you can only rely on subjective opinions, and an evaluation that stems from self-interest. When self-interest rules, responsibility gives way to narcissistic, manipulative, and power-driven behavior—the enemy of productive and innovative talent.

Studies conducted by our research group with the American Management Association and MIT in the 1980s and 1990s revealed an interesting fact: Organizations that feed narcissistic tendencies through strategies such as employee satisfaction studies, which tend to focus on employee benefits to the exclusion of responsibilities, suffered significantly higher turnover of highly talented people than did organizations who based their measurements on responsibility. The lesson: *Achievement measured by self-interest drives talent away; achievement measured in terms of responsibility attracts and holds talent in place.*

The recent infatuation with so-called 360 degree evaluations illustrates the point. Using a 360 process, an organization focuses on how peers and superiors evaluate a person's performance. In follow-up studies we conducted for this book in 2005, we found that in companies experimenting with a 360 evaluation process, 78 percent of their TalentLeaders reported such serious concerns with the process that they had decided to abandon it.

The Top Five Problems with 360 Evaluation

#1   The 360 process turns evaluation into a popularity contest, where members of the group hesitate to critique each other lest they receive similar criticism.

#2   The need for group acceptance replaces a proper focus on the company's customers and mission.

#3   Those who find security in the group tend to ostracize outstanding performers.

#4   Measures of overall performance, including quality, service, and financial metrics, gradually decline over time.

#5   Outstanding performers leave the organization at triple the usual rate, only to be replaced by people more acceptable to the group.

How do you solve such problems? How do you create an evaluation system that strengthens an organization's ability to retain and attract the talent needed to succeed in today's intensely competitive economy? Barbara Wolfe, vice president for human resources of Lenox Hill Hospital in New York City during the 1990s, prodded us to answer that question. The answer, it turned out, propelled Lenox Hill to become a beacon of excellence in its industry.

Strengthening Evaluation

Barbara and her organization had participated in earlier studies on evaluation, but a time came when Lenox Hill needed to *apply* what we had all learned. As Barbara reports: "The most significant finding of the studies was that responsibility, being part of something that ennobles your life and gives it meaning, is the most important performance criterion. You've got to evaluate responsibility and what makes it possible at every level of the organization. You can't have different evaluations for different levels, subsidiaries, divisions, departments, or the individuals who work in them. The core of what you're measuring must be the same for everyone, or you risk organizational schizophrenia. The essence of what we learned can be summarized by the axiom 'measure responsibility, not self-interest.'" Okay. That made sense. But what could we *do* about it?

Lenox, struggling with a corporate-wide transformation and reorganization effort brought on by major financial and labor challenges, had come to a crisis point, with self-immolation and chaos looming ahead. Unless we mobilized and focused the most committed and responsible members of the organization, Lenox Hill could go down in flames.

We began by simplifying the questions on everyone's mind: "Why am I here?" and "What will happen to me?" Simple questions, perhaps, but ones that required rather complex analysis to answer. In the end, all our analysis resulted in five valuable lessons.

Lesson 1:
Include Everyone, from the CEO to Frontline Employees

First and foremost, the analysis led Barbara to insist that questions about the organization's core mission, and everyone's role fulfilling that mission, involve everyone from the board to the frontlines. Many of Lenox's people found that insistence more than inconvenient. However, since she had won everyone's respect over the years, everyone paid attention and agreed to form a "Knesset" composed of representatives from the board and sixty-seven other categories of paid and volunteer workers. This group would address the issues of mission and evaluation. At first, the tired old arguments that differences, not similarities, characterize worker categories almost sidetracked the whole project. Professionals, the logic went, differed radically from nonprofessionals; technical staff and service staff shared few commonalities; clinical and scientific people went their own ways; and anyone paid on merit could not understand those with union contracts. What a jumble of interests!

Aristocrat or Worker?

However, at about that time, James Fallows had just published his important book, *More Like Us*, about core issues affecting North American success in the global economy. I asked Mr. Fallows to speak to our "Knesset" about his book, wherein he described the greatest threat to American society as the arrogance of a new and threatening elite, the "professional aristocrat." This elite consisted of the 50-million-plus American and Canadian workers who draw their identity from degrees and licensure (PhDs, MDs, JDs, MBAs, PEs, and so on). They had grown to believe that their credentials entitled them to certain status and financial rights. They assumed they deserved special consideration, an attitude that sent one clear and dangerous message: self-interest trumps responsibility.

During the convocation's question-and-answer period, an internationally prominent physician and Cornell faculty member teaching at Lenox asked, "Why should I care about such a pedestrian issue as evaluation?" Fallows answered, "Maybe you shouldn't care. Let me ask you, and everyone here, a question: Are you aristocrats or workers? If you do not need your paycheck, you are an aristocrat. But, if you do need your paycheck . . . you are a worker. . . . And, if you are a worker, then you and your work are subordinate to the larger work mission that justifies membership in this organization and requires everyone to hold themselves, and others, accountable. With this in mind," Fallows continued, "let me ask, who among you is an aristocrat? Please raise your hand and claim your place of privilege."

No one raised a hand. At first, you could hear a fly buzz in the back of the room. Then, the chairman of surgery, another celebrated physician, stood and said, "You've got us. Point taken. You have appropriately, if painfully, made us aware of our responsibility. Before we ask our employees to give up or change their jobs, we need to ask every physician and other worker whether he or she is fulfilling their responsibility."

I've witnessed similar reactions countless times when a diverse group grapples with the issue of mission responsibility. The results of such discussions, like those at Lenox Hill, cascade down and across the whole organization, uniting the organization in a way self-interest never can.

The Union Factor

Shortly after the convocation, several labor union leaders, accompanied by the Reverend Jesse Jackson, were collaborating in a New York walk for worker rights. As they arrived at Lenox Hill, Barbara Wolfe, James Marcus (a managing director at Goldman Sachs and board chair of Lenox's Transformation Committee), Allan Anderson (the CEO), and I asked them to join us in the boardroom to discuss their concerns. They agreed and, as we listened and shared views of current realities, the issue of the evaluation process came up. Rather than protesting that union members should be excluded, all union leaders, as well as Reverend Jackson, saw it as a mutual opportunity to speak to the survival and long-term success of the institution. Mission responsibility, they saw, could ensure more jobs than it would erase.

This experience disproves the common management opinion that holds that union leaders and their members will resist the fundamental responsibilities of citizenship. Regardless of wage and benefit issues, responsibility for performance must extend beyond management. Conversely, involvement in that responsibility brings union employees closer to their colleagues and, thus, to the job security to which the union originally dedicated itself. Responsibility leads to unity, and from unity springs the best performers.

Lesson 2:
Emphasize Need, Mission, Mutual Interest, and Responsibility

Very early on, the conversation in the "Knesset" addressed four basic groups of questions.

First, what need does our organization fulfill? Why does it exist? Should it continue? Initial focus group discussions with workers pinpointed a grave concern about Lenox's ability to survive in its competitive environment. Who worried most about job security and the organization's stability? The most talented people, who, of course, could most easily pursue other career options.

Second, what is our mission? Could we still honestly define it as "leading the industry in patient service and research"?

Third, does everyone understand and share belief in that mission? Do we satisfy a mutual interest? Do people just "do their jobs," or do they see their careers as a vital part of something beyond their own self-interest?

Fourth, what must we do to achieve and fulfill the need, the mission, and the role? How do we define our responsibilities, both individually and as a group?

To answer these questions, we assembled teams to research and develop answers they could present to the full "Knesset" and then to the board for approval or modification. While this represented a visioning activity, the effort focused on evaluation, with the specific goal of coming up with a system that everyone could understand and welcome.

The very process of posing and answering the first three sets of questions created a sense of organization-wide ownership. Regarding the first question, a study of the marketplace revealed a powerful desire by a broad consumer base to use Lenox's services. From the Niklas Sports Institute, made famous by such sports figures as Joe Namath, to the major research-driven heart surgery program, to the performing artists' institute frequented by such stars as Luciano Pavarotti, Lenox enjoyed market presence, panache, and community respect.

The market research affirmed a clear need for Lenox to fulfill its core mission of leading the industry in patient care, teaching, and research. The continuing pursuit of this mission made it possible for talented people to build a career at Lenox, one that engendered strong relationships with a larger community dedicated to mutually shared goals and values. These conclusions did not appear out of thin air. They arose from grueling, intense, at times feisty and contentious discussions that laid a strong foundation for addressing the final question: responsibility.

Again, we formed teams to develop categories and specific examples of responsibilities. Each team also designated associates to research the issue. From an initial array of fifteen categories, the teams distilled five basic responsibilities the organization could measure with a Balanced Scorecard for Mission Performance.

Lesson 3:
Develop a Balanced Scorecard for Mission Performance

As the following graphic illustrates, the Scorecard includes five basic components: mission, service, stewardship, development, and leadership. Its simplicity made it accessible and applicable to *all* stakeholders, whether internal or external, whether board members or frontline service providers. In addition, researchers could use it as an agenda for group evaluations by patients, vendors, and partners in the service network.

Balanced Scorecard for Mission Performance

Let's look closely at how it works. Mission defines the need for service, which in turn requires stewardship to provide the resources required to deliver service. The organization must develop its people and resources to meet the challenges of fulfilling the mission, which requires leadership oversight, guidance, and assessment to maintain continuous alignment with the core mission. Any individual, any team, any company can apply this model to gauge performance (in other words, to measure the fulfillment of responsibility).

Mission

Does the organization understand the core *needs* it should fulfill? Has it defined its *purpose* and reason for existence? Does the mission reflect shared *interest*, and, most especially, has it determined *responsibilities* for service that people can translate into action?

Service

What is service? Do you think of it as a discrete activity carried out by one department, or do you view it as part of something larger? If you consider it in terms of responsibility rather than self-interest, you will understand why Sam Walton called it "an act of shared citizenship." In other words, a customer is not a foreign presence; a customer is a family member, a partner.

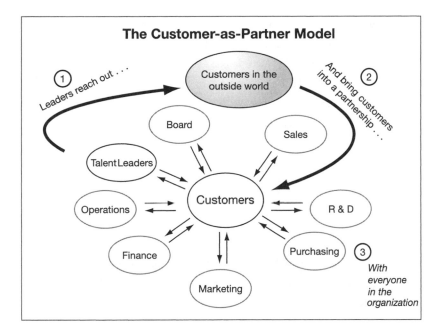

In the case of Lenox Hill Hospital, we thought of our patients as customers. But, at some time in their lives, everyone, whether internal (surgeon) or external (community leader), will find themselves in need of hospital services. The question posed to Lenox's staff was: How would I want to be treated after an accident or during an illness? Lenox's answer: "As a partner; as a person with both rights and responsibilities for the services I receive."

Every stakeholder shares responsibility for doing everything within his or her power to guide and share the journey of service and care. Cooperation, equality, respect, empathy, humility, and

127

courtesy become everyone's watchwords, whether you're chatting with a colleague in a hallway or conducting surgery.

Service is not an abstract concept. It consists of concrete and measurable behaviors. At Lenox we phrased them in terms of a staple question: "Was service responsible, expert, timely, accurate, coordinated, thorough, and sensitive?" The question had applications both internally and externally. You could ask it of a patient's care, and you could ask it of any interaction between team members.

Interestingly, most people find it much easier to measure the fulfillment of the responsibilities with respect to external customers than they do to a colleague down the hall. Therefore, we further developed the question for application to everyday internal team responsibilities: "Do you display respect for each other, maintain appropriate confidentiality, take the initiative to offer assistance, maintain calm and poise in the face of anger, readily share information, and offer and accept guidance?"

Stewardship

What happens if a talented person misses a meeting, incurs a cost overrun, or posts a poor quarterly sales report? Many managers in today's organizations insist that failure to maintain accountability on these issues renders all the other performance measures meaningless. Others argue that such accountability stifles creativity and motivation. Fortunately, responsible pragmatists can intervene by focusing the debate on stewardship. Stewardship is the management and safekeeping of a company's financial and talent assets. Without stewardship of human and material resources, an organization's survival and security lie in constant peril.

For responsible pragmatists, a good steward functions neither as a punisher and corrector, nor as a pal who overlooks transgressions, but as a vigilant guardian of all of an organization's assets, especially its talent. That applies to the steward as well. In any organization, each person needs to be present not only physically but also psychologically. To make this possible, all individuals must align their competencies and the responsibilities with the organization's mission.

The key question for any individual is "Am I in the right place at the right time for the right cost and the right reason?" For the organization as a whole, the question becomes "Are the right people in the right place at the right time for the right cost and the right reason?" In other words, have we aligned individuals and teams to fulfill the mission of the organization, to accept the responsibilities for which we hired them and for which we need their highest achievement?

The answers to these questions, of course, address such performance criteria as efficiency, productivity, and attendance, but they do so within the context of a commitment to service rather than the bottom line. While a company certainly concerns itself with profitability and cost management, such accomplishments naturally derive from alignment. They do not drive it. Service does. Without service, financial success will not materialize. At Lenox Hill, discussions of stewardship, its definition, and its measurement moved from a punitive productivity perspective to one of alignment and individual and team responsibility for the mission.

Growth

No matter what your job, your industry, or your current level of achievement, you can count on one thing: change. Responsibility for meeting its demands belongs to every worker individually and to the organization as a whole. Does the organization demonstrate a commitment to meeting the demands of change by providing resources for growth and development? Do individuals demonstrate initiative in adapting to new realities by improving their skills and knowledge base? Do both demonstrate an understanding of the need for continuous adaptation to changed realities?

Throughout the Talent IQ research we observed an overriding need for involved, committed, and excellent leadership. In research involving more than 1 million employee associates in virtually every type of organization, we heard employees asking for more active involvement and presence in everyday work life. Our earlier book, *Leadership IQ*, emphasized the fact that "every leader works, every worker leads." As the renowned Harvard professor Harry Levine noted, the leader guides and teaches, solves problems, evaluates, and renews. All this requires a connected and committed leader who shares the work experience with her people, a worker who sees herself as a leader in her own sphere of influence, no matter how small.

In similar fashion, those involved in the Lenox project, and all subsequent projects, have declared leadership as the final and determining factor on the Balanced Scorecard for Mission Performance. If organizational leaders do not make themselves actively present in the lives of workers and customers, then the catalyst for service, stewardship, and growth disappears.

Dr. Donna Maria Blancero, former chair of the National Society for Hispanic MBAs, and a leading authority on the history of social change in America, observed, "The genius of pluralistic societies is the dispersion and depth of its leadership power. By contrast with totalitarian economies, where power resides only at the top, power is cascaded throughout the strata of American society, serving as a force multiplier of initiative. Leadership is close to those who work and struggle, giving hope and solving problems. It is not a distant personage wielding the threat of punishment for noncompliance, but a stimulus for individual development and growth. In this way, leadership is democracy and leaders who lead by serving those they lead serve as catalysts for progress."

Drawing upon the unifying power of mission performance, leadership connects all other work systems and makes it possible to create an organizational whole greater than the sum of its parts. Drawing on the early and ongoing Leadership IQ research preceding this project, members of the Lenox and other evaluation projects broke down leadership into eight distinctive role responsibilities, including those of the Selector, Problem-Solver, Protector, Healer, Communicator, Evaluator, Negotiator, and Team Builder.

Eight Leadership Roles

1. **Selector**

   Goal: Select for the customer.

2. **Problem-Solver**

   Goal: Produce results.

3. **Protector**

   Goal: Diagnose and reduce threats to organizational well-being.

4. **Healer**

   Goal: Mend the fabric of organizational life.

5. **Communicator**

   Goal: Build and develop relationships.

6. **Evaluator**

   Goal: Enhance individual performance.

7. **Negotiator**

   Goal: Serve the customer by building consensus on what needs to be done.

8. **Team Builder**

   Goal: Create a whole greater than the sum of its parts.

131

The extent to which a talented person performs these roles provides a strong indication of how well the other components of the Scorecard fit together to fulfill the mission.

Lesson 4:
Translate the Scorecard into an Organization-Wide Evaluation

How do you translate the Scorecard into a practical system for evaluation? First, you use it to conduct an organization-wide assessment completed by internal stakeholders including everyone from board members to those employees on the frontlines of service. The assessment is also completed by external stakeholders, including customers, vendors, and members of the service network. Written, phone, focus group, and online versions can provide an organization with the capacity to conduct a thorough assessment of its mission effectiveness. With more than 300 organizations having used this tool, we know that its five key categories account for virtually all measures of organizational success, including financial, quality, legal, talent retention, and, most important, competitive success.

However, the best benefit of the organization-wide evaluation comes from sharing the results. *Never measure what you won't share.* Transparency always characterizes great companies. Great leadership demands openness in its mission, goals, and criteria for evaluation—openness that stimulates talented people to achieve remarkable results.

In contrast, when an organization withholds or manipulates its Scorecard, the floodgates open for dishonesty, corruption, and failure. Nothing will drive away talent more surely than duplicity and manipulation, and nothing will more surely drive a stake through the heart of an organization.

The Scorecard also lends itself to department or team evaluation. Leaders can use the results in staff meetings to stimulate problem-solving and team building. Rather than offering hearsay information or unreliable data, the leader can focus attention on solid facts, facts on which people can base internal benchmarking comparisons with other departments. Doing so also facilitates the active exchange of information and personnel for role and process improvement. If you include department quality assessment in the organization-wide questionnaire, both internal and external customers can evaluate the quality of their service experience in specific service areas. Such concrete information provides powerful motivation for self-examination, reflection, and improvement.

Of course, in the end it all comes down to the individual. Only by connecting the individual employee to the overall mission can you set the cornerstone of organizational integrity and defeat the threat of hypocrisy and organizational schizophrenia. To accomplish this, the team at Lenox adapted the core criteria from the organization-wide instrument, expanding the concept of stewardship and adding a key section on role-specific skills, which recognized the unique expert skills required for different roles.

For specifics, take a look at the following Individual Performance Appraisal Worksheet. Suppose you are evaluating a sales manager for a chain of electronics stores. You consider Jessica, who is one of your most talented associates, to be destined for a top executive position. Not only do you wish to reward her for all her specific accomplishments, but you also want her to zero in on skills she needs to improve. Let's briskly walk through a general script on how to do that using the worksheet. (The worksheet appears on the following pages.)

Step 1: Prepare for the Evaluation

A week or so before you intend to meet with Jessica to conduct the evaluation, sit down with her and explain how the process works: "Jessica, I'd like to meet with you next Friday to discuss your performance. I think this will be a very positive and constructive opportunity for both of us to examine issues that are really important to your achievement and personal fulfillment, as well as to all of us who work with you and our customers. To prepare for our meeting, I'd like you to do a self-evaluation using the Individual Performance Appraisal Worksheet. I will also complete the worksheet on your performance so that when we get together next week we can compare our perspectives.

Individual Performance Appraisal Worksheet

Directions: Indicate the extent to which the associate demonstrates the following service skills.	Scoring: 1 = Low 5 = High		
	ASSOCIATE	LEADER	FINAL
I. Individual Customer Service Skills (weighting = 20 percent)			
Responsibility—provides ethical service, does not allow personal or organizational issues to interfere with fulfillment of customer needs			
Timeliness—provides responsive service			
Sensitivity—provides emotional support and understanding			
Accuracy—demonstrates clear comprehension of needs			
Coordination—provides service in the right sequence			
Thoroughness—meets the full range of customer needs			
AVERAGE SCORE			
II. Team Service Skills (weighting = 20 percent)			
Respect and courtesy (Contact)			
Awareness of others' needs (Awareness)			
Willingness to become involved (Involvement)			
Empathy and understanding of others' needs (Empathy)			
Willingness to share information (Empowerment)			
Follow-through on work responsibilities (Commitment)			
AVERAGE SCORE			

134

Individual Performance Appraisal Worksheet

III. Stewardship Skills (weighting = 20 percent)

Is present and punctual			
Utilizes financial and material resources efficiently			
AVERAGE SCORE			

IV. Technical Service Skills (weighting = 40 percent)

Skill #1:			
Skill #2:			
Skill #3:			
Skill #4:			
Skill #5:			
AVERAGE SCORE			
TOTAL SCORE: (Add the average score for each section, counting section IV twice, divide by 5)			

V. Comments

VI. Improvement Contract

VI. Signatures

"As you can see, four basic sections address the key areas of direct customer service, service to the team, stewardship, and role-specific technical skills. Regarding the latter, I've inserted job-specific competencies from your job description, as well as other skills we've discussed. If you have others you think are important, add them. If you have questions, raise them when we meet."

Step 2: Conduct the Evaluation

When you get together, start your discussion by comparing your individual perspectives in the following order. First, focus on identical or similar positive scores, at a level of 4 or 5. Begin with a phrase such as, "I agree with you that you provide timely service to customers. Share your thoughts on the issue." At this point you want to establish a positive context for appraisal, a constructive one in which the associate becomes invested, believing it keeps both her and the organization's best interests in mind.

Second, compare the areas with similar but lower scores, from 3 to 1. Here you might begin by saying, "I also agree with you that sharing information with other members of the team could use improvement. What do you think is going on, and how can we do something about it?"

Third, compare the areas where you disagree, but where your own scores are higher. Begin with a comment such as, "Now, let's talk about where we disagree a little. I'm interested to know why you think your technical skills are so low. I've haven't noticed any serious deficiencies."

Fourth, compare those scores where you disagree but where your own scores are lower. Both of you may understandably find this part of the conversation a little more difficult. The associate may hold back, waiting for you to support your score. Thus, you might want to say something like, "Now, let's compare areas where my scores are lower. I'm sure it's no surprise, for example, that I think attendance needs to be improved. I've spoken with you about this before. Your absence during those heavy demand times really put a cramp in our ability to get the job done. What's your view?"

When you've finished reviewing the four areas, pause. Take a breather. After the collaborative comparison, you want to conduct a briefer session during which you share your final assessment. Ask the associate for her comments and respond honestly and respectfully. Next, indicate the improvement you would like to see and enlist the associate's agreement, affixing both of your signatures to the appraisal. You can consult Chapter 5 (The Evaluator) in our earlier book, *Leadership IQ*, for more explanation about how to perfect and apply such a script to evaluation. For now, though, review how Jessica's completed evaluation might look. (The completed sample worksheet appears on the following pages.)

Lesson 5: Differentiate

The great quality guru W. Edwards Deming admonished leaders not to evaluate. "Do not," he said, "separate individuals out from the group through evaluation. It will undermine the team's confidence in itself and isolate the outlier." When I asked him to expand on this admonition at one of the annual dinners held for him and visiting Deming fellows (myself included), at his alma mater, New York University, his answer impressed me. "Do you really mean no one should evaluate individual performance?" I asked.

"Yes and no," he replied. "The key is to not evaluate things that only matter to the individual and have no larger value or meaning to the team and organization. When that is done, the team questions the commitment of leadership to the larger values of the organization and the behaviors that drive organizational success. On the other hand, recognizing achievement in the areas of value to the whole organization strengthens the team and the organization as a whole." The bottom line? Measure responsibility, not self-interest.

Individual Performance Appraisal Worksheet

Directions: Indicate the extent to which the associate demonstrates the following service skills.	Scoring: 1 = Low 5 = High		
	ASSOCIATE	LEADER	FINAL
I. Individual Customer Service Skills (weighting = 20 percent)			
Responsibility—provides ethical service, does not allow personal or organizational issues to interfere with fulfillment of customer needs	5	4	
Timeliness—provides responsive service	5	4	
Sensitivity—provides emotional support and understanding	4	3	
Accuracy—demonstrates clear comprehension of needs	5	4	
Coordination—provides service in the right sequence	5	4	
Thoroughness—meets the full range of customer needs	5	4	
AVERAGE SCORE	*4.8*	*3.8*	
II. Team Service Skills (weighting = 20 percent)			
Respect and courtesy (Contact)	5	4	
Awareness of others' needs (Awareness)	4	4	
Willingness to become involved (Involvement)	5	5	
Empathy and understanding of others' needs (Empathy)	5	4	
Willingness to share information (Empowerment)	3	3	
Follow-through on work responsibilities (Commitment)	5	4	
AVERAGE SCORE	*4.5*	*4*	

Individual Performance Appraisal Worksheet

III. Stewardship Skills (weighting = 20 percent)

Is present and punctual	4	2
Utilizes financial and material resources efficiently	5	5
AVERAGE SCORE	4.5	3.5

IV. Technical Service Skills (weighting = 40 percent)

Skill #1: *Sales Close Skills*	3	4
Skill #2: *Presentation Skills*	4	5
Skill #3: *Prospect and Lead Management*	4	4
Skill #4: *Sales Accounting*	4	5
Skill #5: *Customer Follow-Up*	3	4
AVERAGE SCORE	3.6	4.4
TOTAL SCORE: (Add the average score for each section, counting section IV twice, divide by 5)	4.2	4

V. Comments

I agree with Sal's observations, except that I think my absences were a one-time thing.

Overall, Jessica is a hard-working associate; however, she needs to make more of an effort to reduce her absenteeism, which puts a strain on the rest of the team.

VI. Improvement Contract

Jessica agrees to improve the consistency of her attendance.

VI. Signatures

Jessica Smith (ASSOCIATE)   *Salvatore Bernardini* (MANAGER)

Deming's observation stressed achievement of an organization's mission as the key to its success. That's why measuring it is critical. The record of a high achiever will enhance the identity of the team, not erode it. Thus, recognizing achievement performance through evaluation will help build a culture of responsibility in which service on behalf of the mission becomes the path to success.

At Lenox and at other organizations we have helped, we have always emphasized differentiation and recognition of excellent contributions to mission goals. You must always recognize excellence in service and in all the areas included on the Scorecard, and you must always prepare yourself to confront the improve-or-remove decision whenever service falls short of excellence.

During recent years, we have witnessed a measurable decline in face-to-face accountability between those who serve and those who are served, especially in such critical fields as medicine, law, education, and, most especially, leadership. The inability of customers or citizens to get a straight answer or an objective evaluation causes a potentially catastrophic disconnect between organizations and their stakeholders. In the corporate world, that disconnection drives talent away. Our studies keep coming back to the same fundamental fact: *Nothing accounts for the loss of talented people more than the lack of meaningful evaluation.* Evaluation, more than any other tool, paves the road to improvement.

When IBM reviewed its situation at the beginning of Lou Gerstner's term as CEO, it found that the traditional practice of individual and organizational assessment begun by IBM's founder, Tom Watson Sr., had fallen by the wayside. "Groupthink" had replaced regard for individual innovation, once a hallmark of a company with "Think!" signs on almost every wall.

Regression to the group average had replaced an organization-wide commitment to singular service excellence. Andy Grove, former CEO of Intel and one of the greatest innovators in leadership, notes that evaluation provides a central test of an organization's and individual leader's character. By contrast with the 360 movement, leaders like Grove maintain evaluation as a leader's fiduciary responsibility, with failure to fulfill this responsibility as a ruinous dereliction of duty.

How did Tiger Woods get to the top of his game? The same way you get to Carnegie Hall: practice, practice, practice. The great companies apply that rule to evaluation. Practice, practice, practice—continuous improvement—may not make you perfect, but it will place you on the leading edge, one full stride ahead of competitors. Improve or remove? Measuring responsibility again, and again, and again, will provide the answer.

CHAPTER 7

Improve Team IQ

IN A DYNAMIC WORLD, with flatter and more networked organizations, competitive success depends more than ever on rapid response to change—and the best response often means mobilizing the right people into high-performing teams. An immediate and flexible response can make all the difference between conquering a problem and watching helplessly as it thwarts productivity and results. As a manager, you may have assembled a group of talented problem-solvers, but how do you mesh them into an exceptional team? With Team IQ.

In an effort to isolate the best practices for designing and managing teams, we conducted a specific study of how groups function best together. We learned a lot during the investigation, especially from Ingo Hauptman, project manager, and his team at Hewlett-Packard.

Ingo faced a huge challenge: improve team performance of the company's technical support group (TSG). The TSG, HP's "Delta Force" problem-solvers, directly influenced more than $20 billion in costs annually. Within TSG, a core group of seasoned problem-solvers applied a comprehensive matrix model to bring together key talent from across the corporation in order to meet specific challenges. The process had become a cornerstone of one of the most successful technology corporations in the world. However, it wasn't achieving the results it should have. It had gotten bogged

143

down in a bureaucratic swamp layered with every new team fad under the sun. The teams at HP were spending twice as much time on team process as they were on actual problem-solving. As a result, both quality improvement and the bottom line had gotten stuck in quicksand.

Enter Ingo Hauptman, who was chosen to lead a small group of TSG managers in developing and implementing a new system. As Ingo noted at the time, "Our first task was to decide on a team approach we could use ourselves." Ahmed Misra, a design engineer, agreed. "Yes, and it had to be both simple enough to get us moving and rigorous enough to provide discipline and direction." Another member of the group, Francesca Cortez, added, "While we knew a lot of things impact team effectiveness, we knew that the way in which we thought through a problem was the key and should be our first focus." Yet another group member, Paul Collins, noted, "Sadly, keeping the team happy, learning how to become statisticians, and making sure that any solution we came up with met the team's needs, had gotten in the way of achieving the operational results the team was formed for."

We applied the Pareto Principle right off the bat. There are hundreds of things a team can do, but only a few really determine success, starting with the steps you will take in solving problems. To address the group's central concern—problem-solving—Ingo had invited us to help him conduct a "Team Effectiveness Survey" of TSG associates, other HP teams, and the company's customers.

With the results in hand, Ingo assembled a sort of über-team to sort through all the data and replace the existing "thinking" process with one totally dedicated to solving HP's most pressing problems. Working like forensic anthropologists, digging down through all the layers of techniques that constituted HP team process (Six Sigma, Deming, Juran, early variation engineering, small group dynamics models, and others), Ingo and the group unearthed 1960s videotapes of creative problem-solving sessions that HP had held with NASA. Ingo now shakes his head over how

144

simple it all became. "We found it," he chuckles, "by going back nearly fifty years to the early days of NASA."

Following Russia's October 1957 launch of Sputnik, which was the first satellite sent into space, the United States woke up from its complacency and began rushing to win the space race. It was a daunting challenge that required pulling together all the resources of the Army Ballistic Missile Agency, the Jet Propulsion Labs, and other laboratories and scientists from around the country. Yes, the country possessed all the necessary talent—legendary scientists Wernher von Braun, James Van Allen, Eberhard Rees, E. D. Geissler, Kurt Debus, Helmut Hoelzer, William Pickering, and others—but how could the newly formed National Aeronautics and Space Agency get all the sensitive geniuses functioning as a well-oiled team?

A process originated by Charles Kepner and Benjamin Tregoe, psychologists involved in analyzing how problems are solved, particularly resonated with the scientists. Kepner and Tregoe developed a simple application of the scientific method that channeled the knowledge and energies of individuals through a group process. With it, individuals accustomed to a rather solitary work style could come together to grapple with large and complex challenges. Neil Armstrong's historic step onto the moon's surface in 1969 to pronounce "one small step for [a] man, one giant step for mankind" occurred as a direct result of a problem-solving team management process that encouraged both individual talent and group effort.

Lenny Samuel, another member of Ingo's group, explained: "We had to find a starting point that gave us a solid footing while not burdening us with all the appendages of more recent team theory. Ideas on how to run teams are like a competition . . . where everyone forgets that it's not about the teams, but about the results they are supposed to achieve."

Julianna Penn, the final member of Ingo's group, added, "Because the team process is inevitably complex, we needed a process that was intrinsically simple and straightforward. That's why we chose the basic creative problem-solving process as a seminal path to follow."

Ingo's team adapted the NASA team approach to HP's needs, creating what we called the Talent IQ Team Problem-Solving Process, or TPS for short. Here's an overview of the process, illustrated with excerpts from actual team materials from the HP experience. Over the last several years, many other teams have used it with great success. So can you.

The Talent IQ Team Problem-Solving (TPS) Process

With the ten-step TPS process you can address any challenge assigned to any team. It incorporates a series of filtering questions that separate the wheat from the chaff, steadily guiding the team to a clear solution or the next level of inquiry. The information and insights you develop as you proceed not only provide feedback for revision of earlier steps, but also form the basis for the first steps in the repetition of the process by your team or another.

The TPS Ten-Step Problem-Solving Process

Step 1	Preparation
Step 2	Challenge
Step 3	Define the Situation
Step 4	Problems
Step 5	Solutions
Step 6	Cost-Benefit
Step 7	Plan
Step 8	Authorization
Step 9	Implementation
Step 10	Evaluation and Situation Redefinition

In Step 1, Preparation, you and your team engage in a self-assessment of problem-solving styles. This gives members a chance to get acquainted, and it prepares them for their principal responsibility—thinking!

The team then reviews its "challenge statement," Step 2, which encapsulates the problem and the team's goal. That launches Step 3, Define the Situation. Here you brainstorm the situation and the events that created and surround it. Step 4 moves into a filtering process, where you refine items from the situation list into problems for research and analysis.

At Step 5 you generate ideas for solving or addressing each problem, while at Step 6 you evaluate the acceptability of your proposed solutions through a cost-benefit analysis of their impact on stakeholders affected by the problem. Those solutions that pass this test become part of your plan, Step 7, which you submit through your team leader for authorization and feedback, Step 8. Upon receipt of authorization, implementation (Step 9) commences, followed by an evaluation of results. This evaluation, Step 10, provides data that redefines the situation and initiates a re-examination and new problem-solving cycle.

This step-by-step process propels you toward a solution that works, one that advances the organization's leadership in service, quality, and profitability. To implement it effectively, you should observe the following guidelines:

TPS Guidelines

1. *Base your decisions on data.* While opinions do matter, especially when noting a data deficiency, you should base all analysis on objectively collected data and empirical experience related to the challenge.

2. *Follow the process, but don't hesitate to go back to fill in missing pieces before proceeding.* TPS stresses continuous improvement. When you get blocked at any stage, move back, review and

revise, then press forward. If you can't overcome a block, the blockage itself may deserve a full TPS attack.

3. *Always move forward!* As you make progress, you may uncover other problems. Let other teams tackle them. You cannot solve all problems with a team that is charged with dealing with just one.

4. *Respect diversity in the way people think.* Recognize your preferred method of processing information, and accept the fact that others may do it differently.

5. *Call time out.* Expect occasional tension and disagreement. That does (and should) happen when talented people get together to solve a problem. When it does, pause, take a deep breath, talk things over calmly. To help bridge differences, let humor work its way into the conversation.

6. *Strive for consensus, not compromise.* Consensus seeks a solution that is greater than the sum of the parts. Compromise settles for the path of least resistance. When it's raining problems, compromise makes a poor umbrella.

7. *Test your ideas in terms of utility and acceptance to stakeholders.* No solution will work if a key stakeholder refuses to accept it or it doesn't pass a cost-benefit test. Evaluate the results. Results may mark the end of a certain quest, but they also mark the beginning of another.

8. *Prepare your successors to take up the next challenge defined by your efforts.* Maintain complete and well-organized information files, but keep them as clear and concise as possible.

9. *Keep implementation in mind.* You may or may not be assigned the implementation phase, but the team does not achieve its goal until someone takes action and gets results.

10. *Practice humility.* Ask for help and utilize a team coach to get you started on the right track or realigned with the proper protocol.

Because HP has created a team-driven environment, newly assembled teams usually include members who have experience using the old system. That fact made it all the more important that the new process was easy to learn and easy to apply. When the company finally adopted the TPS process, members of Ingo's team served as coaches, helping to install and refine the process throughout the organization. In our studies of other organizations, we have found that the use of coaches can make a big difference in terms of rapid response to problems.

Implementing the Team Problem-Solving Process: A Case Study

Let's see how you can apply these guidelines, by reviewing excerpts from the search by Ingo Hauptman's team for a better problem-solving approach. His team developed, tested, and revised the model as they went, recording the results along the way for use in teaching other teams how to use it. Studying this story will help you learn it, too.

The HP team included Ingo Hauptmann, chair; Paul Collins; Francesca Cortez; Ahmed Misra; Julianna Penn; and Lenny Samuel. You'll hear from them as their story unfolds.

Step 1: Preparation—Identify Your Problem-Solving Style

Before doing anything else, pause and assess your personal problem-solving style, and those of your colleagues on the team. How you process information influences how you generate and select data. What tendencies, strengths, and deficiencies does your individual and collective profile suggest? Discuss your results, and the team's, in open forum. Then, without too much delay, move on to Step 2.

Francesca provided an interesting insight. "One place where we wanted team members to pause and focus on individual and team characteristics was in the area of how they think," she noted.

"A lot of stuff we saw in the team literature was superficial psycho-therapy. It got us sidetracked into areas that didn't belong in this forum. On the other hand, how you process information is very relevant to this process. Also, examining this issue has a humbling and focusing effect that contributes to mutual respect and a realization that how we carry this process out requires more than our individual points of view, regardless of how superior we think it might be. This enables the team to develop a lot of self-awareness, on many levels."

Exercise: Assess Your and the Team's Problem-Solving Style

Research in the neurosciences confirms that how we process information greatly influences our choices, decisions, and general success in meeting work challenges. The Information Processing Grid provides an overview of five general ways in which people process information, with the M-Pathic type representing a more learned and integrated style that results from a conscious effort to include the other four styles in your repertoire. The M-Pathic style is an integrative style that enables you to adopt effective characteristics of other styles on an as-needed basis. The M-Pathic style results from learning and maturity in managing problem-solving and relationships. It is characterized by the ability to tune into others and approach them from an "I want to understand" perspective.

In turn, this allows the other person in a relationship to share information in an unimpeded way. Receipt of such information enables you to develop empathy, which is an ability to understand another's needs and motivation. Such empathy, in turn, makes it possible to adapt your communications to respond accurately to the other person's needs.

This tends to focus and calm the other person who, in turn, begins to reciprocate by beginning to empathize with you. Such reciprocity engages you and the other party in ways that filter out intense and stressful emotions such as anger, fear, and anxiety. The result is the exchange of more accurate and useful information, and the establishment of a reality-centered environment for solving problems. Such an M-Pathic approach to problem-solving and relationships is a cornerstone of Team IQ and is referenced numerous times throughout this book. It is the desired problem-solving state and one to which each individual on the team should aspire and which you, in fact, may already practice in large measure.

However, under stress, even the most multipathic processor tends to draw heavily on deeply engrained tendencies. These are the information-processing and problem-solving styles we learned early on. Only later do we learn and adopt characteristics of the M-Pathic style. Thus, it would be very helpful to know what your more engrained styles are, and the tendencies they might suggest.

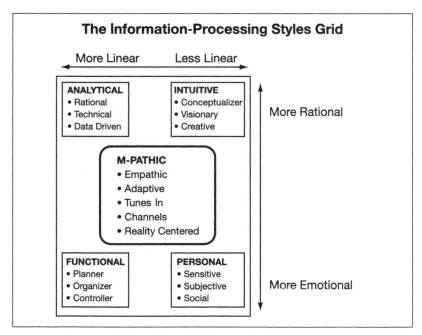

The Information-Processing Styles Grid

More Linear   Less Linear

ANALYTICAL	INTUITIVE
• Rational	• Conceptualizer
• Technical	• Visionary
• Data Driven	• Creative

More Rational

M-PATHIC
• Empathic
• Adaptive
• Tunes In
• Channels
• Reality Centered

FUNCTIONAL	PERSONAL
• Planner	• Sensitive
• Organizer	• Subjective
• Controller	• Social

More Emotional

This exercise will help you and your team explore these styles as well as how you will most likely approach decision-making. Use it to stimulate some self-reflection and, perhaps, some lively group discussion.

Review each of the problem-solving styles. Rank each of the four styles: analytical, intuitive, functional, and personal, from 1 (most like you) to 4 (least like you). Each style includes the positive as well as the negative attributes of that style. You will probably find that no one style describes you perfectly. However, 99.9 percent of us start out from a core position as we evolve our problem-solving style over time. Therefore, try ranking yourself in terms of all four styles. (See the worksheet on the facing page.)

Now you can identify two effective and two ineffective characteristics from the style you ranked number one, and one effective and one ineffective characteristic from the one you ranked number two. Record them in columns labeled "effective" and "ineffective."

After all participants have completed their lists, the team leader can proceed, asking each member to share the styles they ranked first and second, including the specific characteristics they identified. Individuals should be able to explain why these characteristics describe their accustomed approach to problem-solving.

After each individual team member speaks, the team leader can combine all the lists to create an overall profile of the team. Using these results, the leader can facilitate a discussion of how individual and team profiles may affect the TPS process.

"After team members go through this process," explained Lenny, "you notice a settling down and keener awareness that this [initiative] will take some serious effort. These people are motivated and accomplished, or they wouldn't be on the team. However, there is usually a fair degree of unfamiliarity [with each other] and this is a relatively nonthreatening way to meet each other without crossing lines of personal intimacy. Whatever we ask them to do, we want it to be viewed as justified within the context of their work assignment. One of the problems with other team strategies we've used was they crossed the line into domains of the personal not justified by the team's charge. This too often resulted in the whole process becoming bogged down by questions of purpose and possible manipulation."

Problem-Solving Styles Characteristics Worksheet

ANALYTICAL

Effective		Ineffective	
Deliberate		Indecisive	
Prudent		Overcautious	
Weighs alternatives		Overanalytical	
Stabilizing		Unemotional	
Objective		Nondynamic	
Rational		Distrustful	
		Too serious, rigid	
SCORE		SCORE	

INTUITIVE

Effective		Ineffective	
Original		Unrealistic	
Imaginative		Disorganized	
Creative		"Out there"	
"Big picture"		Scattered	
Charismatic		Naive	
Idealistic		Impractical	
Intellectually tenacious		Dogmatic	
Ideological			
SCORE		SCORE	

FUNCTIONAL

Effective		Ineffective	
Pragmatic		Doesn't see long-range	
Assertive, directional		Status seeking, self-involved	
Results-oriented		Acts first, then thinks	
Objective		Controlled and controlling	
Competitive		Domineering	
Confident		Arrogant	
SCORE		SCORE	

PERSONAL

Effective		Ineffective	
Spontaneous		Impulsive	
Persuasive		Manipulative	
Empathic		Overpersonalizes	
Focuses on values		Sentimental	
Probing		Postponing/procrastinates	
Introspective		Guilt-ridden	
Draws out others' feelings		Stirs up conflict	
Loyal		Subjective	
SCORE		SCORE	

Step 2: Accept the Challenge

Your team should review a clear and concise challenge statement to launch the process. It includes a basic goal and a context for meeting it. This authorizes your team to commence work. The HP team received this challenge statement:

Team Challenge Statement for the TPS Process Design Team

"Your team will develop a team problem-solving process for HP that more efficiently and effectively utilizes human capital and other resources to achieve Corporate Mission goals of improved quality, service, and profitability."

Ingo described it this way: "The challenge or problem statement is a way to get things launched without locking the team into an operational solution that may prove to be off the mark. Too often in the literature and in our previous experiences, the goal a team was charged with proved to not be what they should have been focusing on. This blocked them, led to controversy with management, and wasted time and effort."

Step 3: Describe the Situation

Here the team wants to develop a broad understanding of factors that have contributed to the problem. Brainstorm everything you and your team know about the situation. This means searching across the landscape of your knowledge and experience to pinpoint all the events that contributed to the problem. Do not assign a value to the factors; simply list them. Here, more *is* better. List both what you do and don't know, such as your and others' observations and questions, data on the subject, missing information you will need to add, and results from previous efforts to address the problem, as well as outcomes, issues, and other problems and plans that might have affected the problem. Throughout the later steps of the process, keep checking back to add to the situation list and amend the other steps accordingly. This provides a relatively efficient way to record team proceedings for future reference and later teams.

Excerpts from the TPS Process Design Team's Situation List

(selected from more than 100 different situation statements)

- Previous team process bogged down.
- Team members resented sidetracks into personal domains.
- Process took too long to get to actual problem-solving.
  - Everyone spent too much time preparing to prepare.
  - Teams rarely produced concrete results on predictable schedule.
- Absence of team members from assignments meant core assignments were left undone or overburdened others.
- The team process resulted in little ROI with no real accountability.
- People are starting to view teams as a career dead-end (hard to attract good team members).
- The need to assemble teams with right expertise even greater than before.
- People from different areas are brought together with little if any prior relationship.
- Team members need a way to learn about each other without getting bogged down in unproductive sidebar activities.

Step 4: Develop Problem Statements

155

When you have compiled a comprehensive situation list, cluster related items by combining, pruning, or reinforcing the importance of key issues. Then, turn those clustered issues into problem statements that simplify and unify the clustered issues as much as possible.

Excerpts from the TPS Team's Problem Statements

- *Problem 1.* The previous team system failed to produce timely, cost-effective results.
- *Problem 2.* The previous team system demotivated talented staff by including too much irrelevant bureaucratic work.
- *Problem 3.* Team members are too often strangers with too little knowledge of each other and their work methods.

Debate the phrasing and priority of the problem statements until they reflect the status of what the team does or does not know and thinks should or should not be done to solve the problem. Select the top five problem statements for use going forward. These should reflect the concerns raised in the original challenge statement to the team.

Step 5: Develop Solutions

Use the problem statement as a guide to brainstorm potential solutions. Then, just as you clustered situation statements together, cluster potential solutions together for each problem, shaping them into specific problem solution statements.

Excerpts from TPS Team Proceedings

- *Problem 1.* Develop a team process that produces timely, cost saving results by searching for examples from inside and outside the HP experience that have achieved both.
- *Problem 2.* Motivate team members by identifying a process from the Problem 1 search that keeps team members, especially highly talented ones, focused on problem-solving with a minimum of bureaucratic distraction.
- *Problem 3.* Introduce team members to each other through creative initial interaction.

As Lenny noted, "This is where the team starts to feel the pinch of decision-making. Here they start to see that the solution to one or two problems has within it the seeds to solve others, and so they begin to establish priorities from the problem statements that prepare them for the planning phase."

Step 6: Perform a Cost-Benefit Analysis

A cost-benefit analysis should answer two basic questions: First, what will be the implementation cost (including personnel, equipment, facilities, and so on)? Second, what benefits will it deliver in terms of return on the investment of personnel, equipment, and facilities? Will it achieve specific savings as it solves the problem? If so, subtract savings from overall costs to achieve a projection of the cost benefits.

If the situation passes the cost-benefit test (that is, it delivers results that outweigh the costs), fine-tune the plan and submit it for authorization through your team leader. If it doesn't pass the test, examine whether you've underestimated the value of the plan or can creatively reduce implementation costs without compromising results. Review the flow of your team problem-solving, revising and expanding as needed. If you cannot get better answers, repeat the process, approaching the problem from a fresh perspective.

Excerpt from TPS Team Proceedings Cost-Benefit Analysis

Per the attached spreadsheet, personnel and resource costs for conducting a six-week test of the new team problem-solving system will be $55,000 for oversight by the designers of the new system and $140,000 for the team selected to test it out in redesigning the Printer Design Process. Should the team reach its goal of generating $400,715 in increased revenue, the company will earn $205,715 in profits the first year and over $1,000,000 over 5 years.

As Ingo noted, "The cost-benefit review is often where things finally take on substance. Previously, teams submitted what were essentially suggestions without any basis in cost-benefit reality. The result was often rejection or, if it slipped by and received authorization, it led to the implementation of a plan that failed. In both cases, the team also failed, with increasingly negative results for everyone involved."

Step 7: Create a Plan

Select the most viable solutions and propose a plan for carrying them out. This plan should address the question, "Who will do what, by when, with what resources?" Here the team makes specific recommendations they think will best conquer the challenge.

Excerpt from the TPS Plan Statement

Our plan will be to create a team process that will produce timely, cost-positive results, motivate employees, and prepare team members to work with each other. To achieve this, members of the team will be assigned to research team literature and experiences from both within and outside the company over a two-week period. At the end of two weeks, the team will meet again to sort through the results and make follow-up assignments to achieve clarification and create specific design options for implementation. The leader shall coordinate individual and subgroup meetings, bringing the whole team together to decide on a final recommendation within four weeks from initial launch. Following the decision, members will prepare and submit a final version and records of proceedings for authorization. Following authorization and accompanying feedback, the team will make changes in advance of implementation.

"This is a very simple plan, but makes a point," observed Ahmed. "A plan has to lay out what is going to happen to whom, by whom, why, when, and how. Most plans are quite detailed, and we train the teams to think through how they would actually implement the plan themselves and to include specific implementation steps as descriptive material after the basic plan statement. Most often, we ask the team that creates the plan to implement it, if it is acceptable and gets authorization."

Step 8: Seek Authorization

In Step 8, the team submits its final recommendation, complete with the cost-benefit analysis and a specific plan for implementation. These documents (and/or a formal presentation) will enable management to make a red-light/green-light decision. If they disapprove, the process will go back to square one with the same or another team. If they approve the plan, this or another team will move to the implementation step.

"An important dimension to the authorization process is the feedback you get from above," noted Paul. "Previously, because things were so complex and took so long in moving to a meaningful plan, teams typically did not get much more back than yes or no. Now, as in our case, you get a serious response. Ours was an insistence that members of the team followed implementation all the way through by serving as coaches to teams using the new process."

Step 9: Implement the Solution

Management may assign your team to implement the plan, or it may decide to assemble a new team to do so. In the HP case, Ingo's team took responsibility for installing the TPS process by teaching a new team how to use it to tackle the company's most pressing challenge: printer design reengineering.

"We worked with the new team all the way through the process. And, it's a good thing we did," said Francesca. "Not because there

159

were problems, but because we saw you really could get something done and we wanted to make sure we understood why it worked. The key is momentum. When you start out with your preparation focusing on how you think and problem-solve, everybody seems to understand that that is why they are there. There are no psychological games. But, there is an intensive emphasis on testing your ability to think and problem-solve. The result is results."

Step 10: Evaluate Results

Within 90 to 120 days of implementation of the plan, the team should conduct a formal evaluation to determine whether the cost-benefit projections submitted to justify implementation have been met. Examine the results with a cold eye. Do they fall below, match, or exceed expectations? Is plan implementation on track, or is a course correction required? We often suggest that the evaluation include the principles presented in Chapter 6, Measure Responsibility. If results fail to meet expectations, your team or a new one will probably repeat the process until they do.

Excerpt from TPS Team Proceedings

A two-step evaluation procedure was employed for the TPS Process Design Team's efforts. First, a new team was formed to accept the Charge of Redesigning the Printer Design Process. The team completed its work in five weeks, one week ahead of schedule. The results were authorized for implementation with an evaluation conducted 90 days after initial implementation. Early results confirmed that the cost-benefit projections proposed by the TPS and reasserted by the Printer Design Process Team were achieved. In fact, if the Printer Redesign Group can sustain initial results, annual results will exceed initial projections by 100 percent.

Ingo summarized the evaluation process by noting that "it is a transparent, straightforward process that works. Rather than make up artificial criteria for evaluation, we took the goals and objectives that the Printer Redesign Group was obliged to achieve. We, that is, the TPS and the Printer Redesign Team, aligned our objectives with those of the work group we were charged to help. Thus, the criteria for evaluation are the very same as the objectives set from the very beginning. Doing it this way keeps us all focused on the fact that we are part of something very tangible."

Of course, all the issues that surround the concept of teams could inspire its own book, but in our experience, focusing on team problem-solving automatically addresses many of those issues, from leadership and motivation to improving or removing underachieving individuals. However, one team issue does, we think, deserve a special chapter of its own: managing conflict.

CHAPTER 8

Manage Conflict—Now!

WHY MUST CONFLICT be addressed immediately and decisively? Conflict management consultant Lynne Eisaguirre shares a story that illustrates why.

"A group of eight people gather around a conference table to discuss the merits of several companies that are vying to become the new IT provider for the division. Not ten minutes into the meeting, things turn ugly. The accounting manager sulks because billing functions aren't even among the top ten system features being evaluated. The IT manager is indignant that the operations people keep interrupting her presentation to explain the kinds of reports they need in order to measure performance against budget. When the IT manager directs the discussion in favor of a particular system, the vice president of operations lashes out that his staff is not getting the chance to participate in the selection process. The CEO detaches himself from the fray. The meeting ends in disarray and hostility.

"And the person who contributes to the deadlock? The CEO. His style of conflict resolution is to avoid it. He refuses to assume leadership in conflict. As a result, not only do conflicts continue to fester without resolution, but his organization loses its creative edge while his most innovative employees resign in disgust at the lack of forward progress on their projects."

163

Conflict is no longer the exception; it's the norm. As Sheri Archangelski, CFO of Exeter Professional Staffing, observes, "Conflict has moved from being an occasional event to a constant concern. It's always just beneath the surface. There's an edginess that's ever present today. It's definitely different than it was ten and certainly twenty years ago. While underlying interpersonal drivers of conflict remain essentially the same, the more rapid cycles of conflict and increasing intensity create a very new and more threatening work environment. Even more of a problem is that our leaders, from line management to teams, aren't prepared for it. They see themselves as people who want to get things done, not mess around with people who lash out at others because of a crisis of self-control. Yet, they're the ones who *must* deal with it."

Our Talent IQ research underscores the fact that highly talented people, more than average performers, find themselves in conflict with others. The reason? In the process of moving forward, they set examples that typically threaten affiliators and power players less interested in achievement. This, by itself, need not be a threat. However, when a culture of achievement has either not been advanced by management, or individual managers themselves have advanced through affiliation and power brokering, then achievers do not receive the support they need. The absence of such support is viewed by affiliators and power brokers as a signal to attack, leading to conflict.

Ninety-three percent of TalentLeaders listed conflict management as their number one fear. Furthermore, 87 percent considered themselves less than adequately prepared to deal with it.

When the two talented employees collide, collaborative and professional conduct may fall by the wayside as frustration, injured pride, and anxiety take over. When such emotions do take over, a conflict can easily escalate to the point where it requires immediate and decisive intervention. If you don't choose to manage it immediately, the negative energy it produces can ripple through the organization with the destructive force of a Category 3 hurricane.

James Cullen, J.D., chair and managing partner of MacDonald Illig, one of Pennsylvania's most prominent legal firms, insists that a minute of prevention is worth an hour of intervention: "We see clients unprepared to deal with conflict on the individual level, with the result that it escalates out of all proportion to what it had to be. Early and direct intervention by the leader in charge would prevent the vast majority of the conflicts that create business turmoil."

So, why do so few leaders know how to manage conflict? Lourdes Hassler, CEO of the National Society for Hispanic MBAs, chalks it up to the education and development of leaders: "The professional preparation of our leaders often focuses on collegial interaction, facilitation, and win-win relationships to the point that a fully realistic picture of leadership's responsibilities isn't presented."

To better understand the issues ourselves, we asked TalentLeaders to rank conflict situations in terms of their frequency and difficulty. They cited the following three types of situations, which occur in organizations 90 percent of the time:

1. *The Triad*—Two people put the leader in the middle of the conflict.
2. *The Passive Aggressor*—A person who attacks others indirectly by spreading gossip and discontent.
3. *The Disruptor*—A person who tends to deliver emotion-laden attacks in a variety of guises, including the Gossip, the Bomber, the Bully, or the Manipulator, as covered in Chapter 4.

Fortunately, our research uncovered effective ways to deal with these three potentially damaging situations. By employing the right skills at the right time, you can transform threatening situations into opportunities for creating greater individual and team focus on purpose and responsibility.

The Eleven Commandments of Conflict Management

We are going to address each of these three conflict situations through case studies drawn from the Talent IQ research. However, before doing so, consider the following Eleven Commandments of Conflict Management that were documented by the research. They are the axioms that TalentLeaders used to guide their behavior in dealing effectively with very intense and difficult conflict challenges.

#1: *Do it now.*

Conflict can spread like an infectious disease. Each hour, day, or week you avoid dealing with it, it *will* grow. Eventually it will systemically shut down your team—and organization—to the point that it requires a more massive intervention. This can include disciplinary action up to, and including, the removal of the conflicting party or parties. Be aware of this, though: conflict is highly viral in nature. Leaders who don't manage conflict often find their own performance called into question—especially when that conflict leads to diminished productivity and staff attrition. If you don't deal with conflict, it could eventually deal you out of your position.

#2: *Define conflict not as a problem but as an opportunity for improvement.*

When you resolve a conflict, you can do so in a way that clarifies and reinforces individual and team responsibility for achieving the organization's mission. Conflict contains energy, energy that can wreak havoc, but energy that can also be channeled to good use.

#3: *Assess the risk personally.*

Do not delegate responsibility for conflict management because, if you do, you cannot take full advantage of the opportunity to establish your mark as a leader. Leaders who avoid assessing the challenge personally increase the odds of losing legitimacy in the eyes of their subordinates and colleagues and, eventually, their own failure and termination.

#4: But do not clean up the mess yourself.

The leader's job is to address the source of the conflict, not to clean up the performance mess left by conflicting parties. Do not jump in to save the day by taking on their work responsibilities. Rather than being seen as a hero, the leader is seen as an avoider and martyr, performing a coverup to avoid leadership responsibility. Make assumption of responsibility central to resolution of the conflict. Remember, conflict is about performance, *not* about personal likes and dislikes.

And, it is often initiated precisely to avoid responsibility for performance. However, leaders must adhere to their core fiduciary responsibility by protecting the customer and the organization's people and resources—and, thus, hold those in conflict responsible for cleaning up the mess created by it.

#5: Do not take sides.

Doing so validates one party over another. Yes, someone may be at fault, but you must gather all the pertinent information about a situation before you make an improve-or-remove decision. Again, responsibility must take a back seat to self-interest.

#6: Guard against any misrepresentation of your intent and interests.

167

Correct any misrepresentations or false charges immediately. Never rely on others to correct falsehoods, or expect that they will go away on their own. Conflict can bring out bad behavior, including the ever-popular "smear the boss" campaign. Lies and innuendo, like a cancer, will metastasize if you don't excise them early.

#7: *Focus on one conflict at a time.*

Simultaneously acting on multiple conflicts dissipates your energy and focus. While one conflict can create a chain reaction, igniting others, the resolution of one conflict can send a clear signal to other people as to how you will handle their situations. Rather than putting themselves through the process, those who are igniting conflict may change their tone on their own.

#8: *Intervene with a minimum of fanfare.*

Try to minimize exposure of the problem to others. Keep the conflict confined to one-on-one and small group discussions. Once again, you want to isolate and treat the cause of the conflict, not all the symptoms that may be running rampant through the organization.

#9: *Insist that the conflicting parties accept appropriate responsibility.*

After addressing each individual involved in the conflict privately, sort out who should own what, and then encourage each individual to acknowledge that fact.

#10: *Resolve the conflict in favor of the customer and your organization's mission.*

Do not, under any circumstance, accord victory to one party over another. Everyone in your organization—most especially you—works for the customer and the company's mission. If you declare victory of one party over another, then you imply favoritism and an inclination to serve special interests.

#11: *Never fear conflict.*

On the other hand, as Lynne Eisaguirre argues, respect the power of a good fight to make people and their organizations stronger.

Now, let's apply these principles to the three major types of conflict: the Triad, the Passive Aggressor, and the Disruptor.

Managing Triad Conflict

Every parent with two or more children has faced the situation in which one child complains to the parent about the other sibling. Often, both children use the parent to complain about the other at the same time. The situation among adults is not much different, though the stakes are usually much higher and the consequences of managing the conflict ineffectively can also be much more severe and not always redeemable.

Triad conflict is especially dangerous because it is ubiquitous, occurring virtually everywhere, regardless of setting or location. The good news is that the solution is also fairly universal. It involves the recognition of basic principles of how to manage the situation and a script for translating those principles into action. Both the principles and script provide a foundation skill set on which to build as you move through the other conflict situations that you may encounter.

To illustrate the effective management of a Triad conflict, consider the case of benchmark TalentLeader Carlos Ortiz, principal and general manager of a worldwide construction firm. Carlos routinely works with multinational work teams in South America, Asia, and the Middle East who literally don't speak the same language. Over the years, he has learned the importance of assessing and, if necessary, responding rapidly to situations that could actually explode into physical conflict. As a result, he's become a master at *managing conflict—now!*

In the sample dialogue on the following pages, notice how he observes the 11 Commandments discussed earlier as he uses them in conjunction with the following ten-step process to resolve conflict on a bridge construction project in Mexico City.

A Ten-Step Conflict Resolution Process

Step 1	Listen to Party A
Step 2	Observe
Step 3	Listen to Party B
Step 4	Problem-solve with Party B
Step 5	Meet with Parties A and B
Step 6	Clarify each party's position
Step 7	Guide dialogue
Step 8	Search for a solution
Step 9	Seek consensus
Step 10	Implement a decision

Carlos approaches Bon Wing Chiu, the site foreman:

Carlos: Good morning, Bon. Is your crew ready to pour the pier footing this morning? (*Carlos initiates contact at Step 1. The pier he refers to supports the bridge platform over the San Miguel river in the northeastern part of the city.*)

Bon: No, Carlos, we're not ready, as usual. And, you can blame Vered [Rabia]'s form construction team for that. They were supposed to have it done yesterday, but they goofed off. We work like dogs and they never pull their weight.

170

Carlos: I understand you're angry, Bon, but let's just focus on the pier for the moment. Will you be able to pour in an hour?

Bon: Yes. But I want you to know we're going to fall behind schedule if those guys don't get their act together.

Carlos: I hear you, Bon, but let's just focus on the pier right now. Okay? (*Carlos acknowledges Bon's concern but focuses the conversation on the work at hand for two reasons. First, he wants to focus energy on meeting customer goals. And second, he wants to assess the situation himself. He observes Bon's preparation—Step 2—while he carries out some administrative duties. He approaches Bon again— Step 3—an hour later.*)

Carlos: Bon, are you ready to pour the pier yet?

Bon: Just starting. We'll make it, Carlos. I'm telling you, Vered is a screwup and you'd better do something.

Carlos: I understand your position.

Bon: That's what you said before. Are you going to do something or not? My team is the one that suffers when Vered doesn't do his job.

Carlos: Bon, I did hear you and I understand you're angry at Vered. Your job is to pour concrete and tell me about any problems you might have. You did that. Now it's my problem. Let me handle my job and you do yours, okay? You concentrate on pouring the pier; I don't want anybody getting hurt. All right? (*Carlos forcefully defines his job responsibilities and establishes his own authority to deal with Vered. At the same time he focuses Bon on the task at hand.*)

Bon: Yeah, all right. (*Carlos sees that the conflict has not extinguished itself and knows he must get to the bottom of it quickly. He also realizes he must approach Vered—Step 4—who has been under a lot of pressure to maintain a schedule himself.*)

Carlos: Vered, got a minute?

Vered: Oh, hi, Carlos. Yeah, but only a minute. We're busy as hell.

Carlos: Tell me about it. What's your team doing today, and is there anything that could get in the way of getting it done? (*Carlos approaches Vered—Step 4—asking about To-Do(s) and roadblocks. He does not mention the conflict yet, since he wants to assess Vered's situation objectively. Raising it as an entry question would contaminate the situation with emotion and raise questions about Carlos's own integrity.*)

Vered: Well, we've got some form reconstruction problems. Bon's crew has been having trouble transporting the concrete to the pier site so they've jerry-built a bridge across the forms we constructed. I understand his problem, but it's knocking the hell out of the forms. So we have to go back and repair them, which slows us up.

Carlos: I see. Did you know that Bon's concerned about the delays? (*Carlos touches on the conflict.*)

Vered: He's concerned? I'm the one taking the hit.

Carlos: Well, there's got to be a simple solution to the problem. Tell you what, meet me at the trailer for lunch. We'll get Bon there, too. (*Carlos calls a meeting with both parties—Step 5—at the trailer that serves as a field office, where he can clarify each party's situation—Step 6. All three convene for lunch.*)

Carlos: Vered, Bon, thanks for coming. I know both of you are under the gun and that we've got some problems to solve if we're going to meet the schedule. Bon, you're worried that Vered's team is going to slow you down by not having the forms ready for pouring, right? (*Carlos immediately takes control of the meeting and sets a positive, problem-solving tone. He separates ego from issue by zeroing in on the practical work problems Bon faces rather than commenting on and thereby reinforcing his anger. He also lets both men know that work, not politics and self-interest, comes first.*)

Bon: Well, slowing me down is a little strong. I'm just concerned about getting my job done.

Carlos: Bon, let me make sure I have this straight. You were late pouring the pier this morning because the forms weren't ready, right?

Bon: Yeah.

Carlos: And you told me that you thought Vered's team was falling behind, right?

Bon: Well, sort of.

Carlos: Look, Bon, it's not sort of. I have a concern here. I need to understand your point of view clearly if I'm going to help. So, tell us, what is it? (*Carlos refuses to be manipulated. He states the problem in nonaccusatory terms—"I have a concern"—and explains why clarification is necessary—"if I'm going to help." He clearly puts responsibility on Bon Wing Chiu's shoulders, where it belongs.*)

Bon: Well, what I meant was that Vered has a heck of a challenge getting the forms constructed, and it worries me that his delay becomes my delay.

Carlos: And that's it, Bon? Nothing else? (*Carlos gives Bon the chance to share his point of view completely before asking Vered's opinion. Typically, the order of questioning follows the order in which the issue arose. Bon raised the issue first, so Bon is addressed before Vered.*) Vered, how do you see things?

Vered: Well, sure we're late. But that's because Bon's crew is beating up our forms by using them as a bridge to get across the pier. We spend half our time reconstructing our original work.

Carlos: How about that, Bon? Were you aware of Vered's problem? *(Carlos moves back and forth to seek clarification, always involving the parties in facing up to their responsibilities for owning the situation. This sets the stage for finding a solution at Step 7.)*

Bon: Oh, I hadn't thought of that. I've been up to here in my own problems. Well, hell, I'm sorry, Vered, but I didn't know how else to transport the cement without laying planks over your forms.

Vered: Well, I know; that's why we didn't complain and just tried to fix them as fast as we could. *(Carlos lets the dialogue flow naturally and then steps in to move it to the next step.)*

Carlos: Both of you guys are working hard, and I want you both to know I appreciate it. I should have seen this coming, too, and now that we all understand the problem, let's find a solution. What about that new scaffolding technique we saw last week? *(Carlos has averted a serious conflict, but he knows that the loss of face for Bon could lead to more anger unless he can help both parties focus on implementing a solution that gives both reason to feel pride. Both men must offer a workable solution to their teams. As in any conflict situation, the workers on both teams are aware of potential conflict. If one leader loses, so does his team, with a likely plunge in morale, productivity, and quality. Carlos also recognizes that he can absorb some of the intensity of the feelings by publicly accepting his own responsibility for the work. Then he offers a plan for moving forward.)*

Bon: That new system we saw in Houston?

Carlos: Yes, that's the one. I can get the plans faxed over by this afternoon. Can you guys get together and study them by noon tomorrow? If you think they can work, I'll support the scaffolding construction tomorrow. What do you say?

Vered: Sure, sounds like a good idea.

Bon: I think so too. I'll be glad to look them over. *(Carlos has moved to consensus—Step 9—reinforcing the importance of collaboration and the need to address the problem head-on. By doing so, he gives both parties an option beyond anger and conflict. To be sure they understand this, he emphasizes the need for action—Step 10.)*

Carlos: Good. Because we need to move forward—together. I want your joint opinion by noon tomorrow, at which time I'll decide whether we can use that system or need to find another solution. I know both of you have a heavy workload this afternoon, so I'll let you get back to work. If you need any help, give me a call. If not, I'll see you tomorrow.

Carlos wraps up the meeting by setting a clear course of direction and refocusing both parties on the work mission rather than the conflict. If Carlos had encountered resistance or an unwillingness on their part to cooperate, he could have adjourned the meeting by saying, "I see we still have some significant differences here. Let's adjourn for today, then get together tomorrow morning at nine, at which time I'll decide what we will do next."

TalentLeaders pursue a collaborative but tough-minded process that focuses each person on his or her respective responsibility to manage conflict and risk. To conclude Carlos's story, the new scaffolding system did work, and Bon and Vered worked closely and effectively to put it in place. TalentLeaders in our study get the same sort of results every day.

Managing the Passive Aggressor

The Passive Aggressor comes in a variety of forms, as identified in Chapter 4, Improve or Remove Talent-on-the-Bubble. However, all passive aggressors tend to avoid direct engagement with those on whom they set their sights, preferring to seed the communication network with criticism, gossip, personal innuendo, and doomsday predictions, including the likely demise of jobs, security, and any form of normalcy. Passive aggressors are particularly dangerous because their action implies a natural defense of, "Who? Me? What did I do? You can't prove a thing!" As a result, the leader may refrain from addressing what everyone silently recognizes as a genuinely serious problem.

Remember when Carlos resolved his Triad conflict? He approached Vered within the context of Vered's routine role as a manager and leader. He did not accuse or prejudge Vered's behavior, but sought to engage him in the normal problem-solving responsibilities of work. Only after collecting information and analyzing it did Carlos move to address the conflict itself. This basic strategy works with the Passive Aggressor, too.

Since the Passive Aggressor's avoidance of direct engagement is a cowardly act, the leader can use that fact to shift the burden of response from those under attack and back to the Passive Aggressor. The leader approaches the Passive Aggressor (PA) within the context of his of her responsibilities and asks for the opportunity to discuss work. If the PA says, "Can't this wait? I'm busy right now." the leader responds, "I understand, things can get hectic. What's going on, and how long is it likely to take?" As the conversation proceeds, the leader can give the PA a pass for the moment, scheduling a meeting at a later time (preferably that same day). If the PA fails to justify postponement, then the leader should ask the PA to join her in her office to chat about work.

Unlike the conflict Carlos resolved, in this case the leader initiates a private discussion. While the rest of the team will not know the details of the conversation—at least not from the leader—everyone else can see that the leader has openly engaged the PA and, by implication, will do so with anyone else. From the PA's point of view, who can object to a "routine" chat about work? Also, regardless of what the PA says afterward, the leader has conveyed a basic message of accountability: "You may try to hide behind gossip, but you can't run away from work responsibilities." During the meeting with the PA, the leader asks four probing questions in a certain order, repeating them over and over until a reasonably informed picture of how the PA spends his or her time emerges and the leader believes that he or she has driven home the point that accountability rules this workplace.

Four Focus Questions

#1	What work do you do?
#2	How much time do you spend working each day?
#3	What interferes with your work?
#4	How much time does interference consume?

Listen to how Rene Stanley, a UPS division manager, handles Passive Aggressors: "I start by saying 'I'd like to ask you four simple questions. They're intended to help me understand your work situation more clearly and for us to have an opportunity to see if we can make it even better.' Then, I ask them to write the questions down on a yellow pad, keeping space between them for answers. I do the same thing myself as I proceed with the interview.

"First I ask, *'What's going on? What work do you do?'* Second, *'How much time does each work item take? How many hours and minutes, down to fifteen-minute blocks?'* Then, I shift gears and ask, *'Now, third, looking at things from a different point of view, what gets in your way? What specific things, like phone interruptions, people interrupting you, tracking down bad information, or having to do work over, causes inefficiency and stress?'* And, fourth, *'How much time does each of these items take?'*

"Often, the PA asks me, 'Why are we doing this? Is something wrong?' I never answer these types of questions, which are only a way for the PA to sidetrack the issue, but rather, respond by saying, *'I understand this may be a bit new to you, but this is a good technique for us [to use] to look at what you have going on here at work and how I might be able to help you. So, let's just stay focused on the simple questions of work and time and discuss the picture of work that emerges.'*

"I'll follow this through until we've got a reasonable start and then ask, *'Do you think this is an accurate picture, or would you like a little private time to consider things more thoroughly? Then let's get back together to see where things stand. I'd like to get to know you and your work better, and this is a good start. Thanks. I'll set up another time in a couple of days.'*

"Then, I always follow through, continuing with the discussion and refining the answers until we both feel it represents a realistic picture of what's going on. Then we have a discussion of what the picture means and how it could be put together differently to produce a more effective and efficient work role."

Rene and others who employ this type of technique note that, with most PAs, it establishes a nonthreatening relationship. Often, that's exactly what the PA craves most: respect and involvement, which occur more easily without the emotional baggage of an accusation. Since fear drives the PA's behavior, you want to do everything you can to dispel fear and anxiety. Once you do that, you can explore underlying attitudinal and competency issues that require improvement. If the PA persists, removal may be the best option.

While you can play variations on this script, it's best to keep it simple. Its very simplicity gives it power to keep people focused on their work and on their responsibility to fulfill the organization's mission. The subject of work provides the most legitimate basis for taking leadership initiative, especially when engaging the Passive Aggressor. Confine discussion to work and issues related to it. You can gracefully move from that platform to a discussion of other, more complex, issues, such as communication and motivation.

Managing the Disruptor

Most leaders find the Disruptor quite difficult to manage. Disruptors come in interesting forms: the Whiner, the Bomber, the Blocker, and the Heckler.

Four Classic Disruptors

The Whiner	Constantly complains
The Bomber	Exhibits anger and hostility
The Blocker	Impedes progress
The Heckler	Argumentative; makes everything a production

To understand the dynamics of these conflict types, as well as to gain further insight into our previous examples, we're going to draw on the behavioral model developed by Eric Berne some fifty years ago and refined as part of contemporary cognitive communication models. In this model, you concentrate on the communication state in which the conflict arises, matching your response to that particular style. Like martial arts defense or attack moves, this model provides a way to analyze the nature of the attack and formulate the best mode of response.

The left side of the model depicts the blending of the four problem-solving and leadership styles we discussed earlier; the right side lists the four classic types of Disruptor. Each type of Disruptor responds best to an approach that takes his or her style into account; each type of leader must take that into consideration as he or she engages a particular Disruptor (see the chart on the following page).

For instance, consider the case of the Bomber, who attacks a colleague with an emotion-laden bomb. "What the hell happened? Why aren't things ready? Another screwup! How many times does this have to happen before we go bankrupt, lose our jobs, kill somebody [or, implicitly, make my life inconvenient, miserable, and more intolerable than it already is, thanks to you, you idiot]?"

In the context of the model, this Disruptor combines some traits of both the Bomber and the Whiner, displaying high levels of the "Critically Aggressive Parent" and the "Needy Whining Child." The parent component expresses authority and asserts "should" and "must" do's. In the adult state, the person seeks

179

dominance and control, while in the child state, the person throws a tantrum.

This Disruptor will respond to engagement by a leader who can apply the right combination of analytical, personal, and intuitive communication. For example, in this particular case, the leader will perhaps get the best results by saying something like, *"I understand your frustration with the lack of results we have right now* [analytical]*, and you certainly have a right to get angry about it* [personal]*. I value your input* [relational]*. Can we take this somewhere private where we can explore some solutions that will make everyone happy* [intuitive]*?"*

Transactional Conflict Model

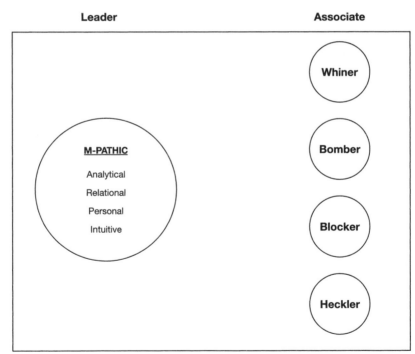

Note how the leader focuses on the work (results), which appeals to the adult, while providing some of the emotional styles the child needs. When it comes to managing high-powered talent that occasionally exhibits disruptive behavior, I've never seen anyone do it better than Dr. James Pepicello, chief medical officer and chief operating officer of one of the top 100 medical centers in the United States. In this intense environment, where life-and-death situations can raise emotional temperatures to the boiling point, maintaining a positive, problem-solving posture makes all the difference in the world, especially when Disruptors raise their ugly heads.

"Fortunately, we have a superb group of physicians and associates. But, when things burst, the response has to be specific and immediate," notes Dr. Pepicello, whose background as a leading trauma and general surgeon for more than twenty years exposed him to all types of stressful situations. "Knowing this, we anticipate and prepare ahead of time. We've schooled all of our leaders in responding to such situations from the 'I understand' state: '*I understand you are upset, and I would like to help you get results. Why don't you start from the beginning and tell me what's on your mind.*'

"Of course," Dr. Pepicello continues, "a flagrant Bomber doesn't always or even usually just stop and cooperate at that initial reaction. And, if he or she doesn't immediately or quickly respond to such adult strategies of response, then it's critically important not to let things get out of hand. In more intense situations, the 'I understand' response can be coupled with '*but, let's adjourn to some place more private where we can discuss things thoroughly.*' For most situations, this is sufficient to bring things under control.

"But, when the Bomber graduates to the level of defiance, then a leader must assert his or her legitimate authority both immediately and compellingly: '*I do understand that you are upset and you might well have interesting reasons for your concerns. But, this is neither the time nor place for such a discussion. Please meet me immediately [or, in the case of a physician or clinician treating a patient] or as soon as you are done, in my office, where I will wait for you.*'

"When you deliver such a message," notes Dr. Pepicello, "it is not only for the subject in conflict, but for those who may be observing the interaction. It's important that you clearly establish

181

who is in control. In the event you are not confident that the now-defiant Bomber can re-establish self-control—which does, however occasionally, happen—indicate that '*I have concerns that you can not maintain self-control in this situation. Therefore, join me in my office immediately.*' Should you sense the need to go beyond this point, it is time to call for security.

"We believe it is vitally important that our leaders know how to handle difficult conflict situations. And, because they are prepared, and feel confident in their ability to manage them, we have very few instances where we need to. Being able to manage conflict is essential to maintaining a calm, constructive environment where associates believe mission will always come first," concludes Dr. Pepicello.

The basic script applies to all four classic types of Disruptors and their various combinations:

"*I understand.*"

"*I know you want to get results.*"

"*I can see why this upsets you.*"

"*Can we work together to solve the problem?*"

If application of the script doesn't work, you might have to utter the final words: "*You're fired.*"

CHAPTER 9

Design a Leadership Talent Map for the Future

WHEN YOU HIRE exceptional talent, 99.9 percent of the time you hire ambition as well. Ambition can make your company—or it can break it. It all depends on how well you develop and channel ambition toward ever-greater responsibility and achievement. Surprisingly, our Talent IQ research revealed that conventional succession planning does not do the job well, a finding that prompted us to design a better method, one we call Leadership Talent Mapping (LTM).

Dennis Chow, chair and CEO of Exsular, a major electronics distributor in the southeastern United States, helped us refine our method. As he puts it, "Of all the challenges we face, making sure we have the right people in the right place at the right time for the right reason and cost, worries us the most. Our staff changes, but so do our needs. However, since we've begun Leadership Talent Mapping, we've been able to turn what was an ever-present fear into a continuously flowing process of team collaboration and visioning for the future. A very important key was changing our thinking from 'succession,' which made people think they were dispensable—perhaps immediately—to 'progression,' which included everyone in moving forward toward new opportunities."

Every organization wrestles with identifying and developing the talent it needs to achieve present and future goals. Talented people drive organizations. Yet, if leaders do not grasp how their talented people do what they do, they can neither align talent for achievement nor plan for future needs.

When Dennis Chow saw his remarkably successful company heading toward an uncertain future because it was not effectively developing its leaders, he asked, "How can we protect our most important asset—our talent? How can we refocus and re-energize them to help us address this new reality so that we can get back on the path to the future in which we are all invested?"

Wayne Randall, vice chair and largest shareholder, noted, "Market conditions, technology changes, and competition are neither our greatest risk nor opportunity. Keeping the talent we've worked so hard to select and retain is. They will manage the risk and take advantage of the opportunity. We must help them to understand how to do that for their and the company's sake. Ours is a shared future. We want them to know that in no uncertain terms, regardless of the blips and dips that occur along the way."

The Succession Trap

All too often, however, when leaders respond to changes such as those threatening Exsular, they resort to traditional succession planning, only to find that they've alienated the very people they need to address both immediate and future challenges. As Dennis Chow pointed out, succession planning implies the eventual loss and replacement of critically important talent. That narrow focus can actually exacerbate the very problem it should solve. As we began recommending a broader approach to 117 client organizations that had historically depended on conventional succession planning, 63 dropped conventional succession planning altogether and 22 discontinued the process in midstream.

Why? As one CEO put it, "We just could not convey our intention clearly. People thought this was another, roundabout way for us to check up on them or eliminate their position." Of the 32 organizations that adhered to a succession planning process, 11

CEOs rated it a success, 7 deemed it adequate, and 14 called it an outright failure. Of all those who declared the process a failure, all cited one overarching reason: *People in line for promotion felt that the process did not adequately involve them.* They felt that the lack of meaningful collaboration robbed them of control over their own destinies and might, in fact, threaten their careers.

While most senior staff saw the final report, even they felt out of the loop. Since a fog of secrecy surrounded the process, many feared that commitments made to them might disappear. Such a fear can drive talent out the door. Organizations can also make a huge mistake if their development of talent focuses too narrowly on immediate productivity and cost effectiveness, without proper attention to individual and team achievement. Such an approach can make people obsessive about short-term results: "If you hit your numbers, great! If not, off with your head!" Obsessed with immediate results, people can't see change coming and can end up missing larger opportunities in the marketplace when they fail to adapt.

When money and productivity issues overrule all else, everyone thinks they are constantly "on-the-bubble," with the axe likely to fall at any moment. For example, leaders of a large corporation who assume they can shut down a manufacturing facility in Ohio with little impact on other facilities are in for a rude surprise when the fallout contaminates and petrifies workers in Oregon and Hong Kong.

Our Talent IQ study proved the point—of the 983 participating organizations, 327 let financial concerns drive re-engineering and restructuring efforts, which reduced their work force from 1.5 percent to 7.5 percent over a six-month period. Ten to twelve months later, those organizations that cut only 1.75 percent of jobs experienced an average 150 percent increase in turnover of their most valuable and talented staff. Those who cut 7.5 percent suffered a 400 percent increase. Fallout? You bet!

When we asked people why they left, more than 80 percent said something like, "Because management had signaled it was time to get out; talented people no longer mattered." As Warren

Bruggeman, former head of GE's Nuclear Energy Division, observed, "When management makes money the immediate reason for change, it signals to everyone that they've panicked and lost their vision. Rather than anticipating and acting proactively by involving those who could help to achieve far-reaching and sustainable results, management too quickly takes out the axe and chops, with typically stupid results."

Leadership Talent Mapping (LTM)

Leading organizations in the Talent IQ study found a way to align their organizations to meet both short- and long-term challenges. They did so by involving their most important personnel in Leadership Talent Mapping, a comprehensive process of analyzing an organization's talent needs for the present and future by matching present and future goals against talent resources and all relevant financial, ownership, market, and competitive realities.

Leadership Talent Mapping is a collaborative problem-solving process driven by self-assessment and an affirmation of the importance of individual and team achievement. It creates a picture of how well individuals, teams, and the whole organization are aligned for achievement of present and future goals. The Leadership Talent Map reveals the path an organization must follow to rebalance and realign its resources to achieve success. With it, individuals can see how they can better apply their talents to achieve personal success while enhancing the productivity and profitability of the organization.

Principles and Practices of Leadership Talent Mapping

The principles and practices of Leadership Talent Mapping resonate with those you have encountered in this book. They provide a checklist for undertaking comprehensive organizational change.

The Leadership Talent Mapping Checklist

❑ **First, define the organization's mission for the present and foreseeable future.**
Do you know who you are and who you want to be? If you feel confident and clear, share your vision. If you're still searching for direction, admit it.

❑ **Second, plan for the future by understanding the present.**
Organizations, like people, develop personalities and practices, some good, some bad. Without understanding these, you cannot construct a sound foundation for the future.

❑ **Third, determine whether the *"right people are in the right place at the right time for the right reason and cost."***
Understand that who you are goes beyond hunches and hearsay. Get the data from those who really know what's going on.

❑ **Fourth, build the data set for your Talent Map from the individual on up.**
Honor and respect your TalentLeaders by making them landmarks on the map. Include others as well, particularly those with emerging potential.

❑ **Fifth, involve individuals in a guided self-assessment process.**
Train managers to coach individuals through the process in a collaborative spirit of growth and development. Remember, you can't prepare for the future if you alienate those who serve in the present.

❑ **Sixth, use a consistent five-part methodology and script for conducting the individual self-assessment.**
As you will see later, a simple but comprehensive five-part protocol for Leadership Talent Mapping emerged from the Talent IQ research. Use it for consistency and reliability.

187

❑ **Seventh, share the results.**
Never publicly measure what you can't or won't share. Both individuals and teams respond more accurately and truthfully when they know that colleagues will be reviewing the results.

❑ **Eighth, compare your results to Talent IQ benchmarks.**
Talent IQ research from across the 983 organizations produced best-practice benchmarks for alignment, focus, efficiency, motivation, complexity, and readiness, among others. Benchmarks provide valuable reference points for understanding your organizational fitness for the future.

❑ **Ninth, initiate problem-solving to improve alignment.**
Build on strengths and take advantage of opportunity. Use techniques from the Team Problem-Solving System discussed in Chapter 8.

❑ **Tenth, repeat the process to maintain focus and measure results.**
Remain constantly vigilant for changes in the assignment that require new Talent Maps.

The Leadership Talent Mapping Five-Part Process

The five-part Leadership Talent Mapping script will help you mine the full range of information. Recall the Problem-Solving Inventory Map that depicted differences in how we process information.

The first two parts of the script relate to the linear analytical and functional styles:

- What do you do? What activities do you carry out in fulfilling your role responsibilities?
- How much time does each activity take?

The next two questions relate to the nonlinear intuitive and personal styles:

- What gets in the way of doing what you should do? What road-blocks and time wasters intrude on your work?
- How much time does each of them take?

The fifth and final set of questions relates to the multipathic style:

- Can you describe opportunities for improving focus and alignment with our mission goals? What problems do you face? How can we solve them?

This guided self-assessment and coaching process poses and re-poses the questions, stimulating observations and insights into daily and weekly work activities. Individuals can ultimately consider the question, "What does this analysis of how you currently spend your time tell us about the opportunities and threats you face in harnessing your full potential?" Such a discussion parallels the coaching protocol explained in Chapter 3. By aggregating the results, the CEO and board, and other leaders and teams, can accurately analyze how effectively the organization is utilizing its talent and how operational leaders might redesign roles, processes, and structures to harness talent more effectively now and in the future.

Leadership Talent Mapping in Action

189

Let's examine three specific examples of how Leadership Talent Mapping works and how you can use it to prepare a Talent Plan as well as use it to enhance individual, team, and organizational performance.

Case #1: Individual Leadership Talent Mapping

This script illustrates how a manager can use Leadership Talent Mapping with an individual to accomplish on-the-spot realignment and focusing. It unfolds in three stages: the encounter, preparing the map, and problem-solving.

Stage 1: The Encounter

Ricardo, or "Ric," the newly appointed manager of one of the Body Shop's busiest stores, has decided to use a Leadership Talent Mapping process with his staff following a seminar he recently attended. However, before he formally launches the process with the full staff, he chooses to test it out first by applying it to an immediate and pressing problem on the sales floor: Two couples, a student, and a family group are all browsing the aisles while one salesperson, Lisa, who should be assisting them, has disappeared into the stockroom, where she has begun assembling a point-of-purchase display.

Ric approaches Lisa.

Ric: Lisa, what's up?

Lisa: I'm putting together a new display.

Ric: Can you take care of that later? We've got a floor full of customers right now. *(Ric quickly identifies and solves an immediate problem—lack of customer service—but knows that he must address the circumstances that caused it.)*

Lisa: Sure.

Ric: Ask me about the display later, when you get a chance. I'm curious about it. *(Ric arranges for a later discussion of the problem.)*

In this brief vignette, we've seen Ric ask the first question: "What are you doing?" Then he interrupts the script in order to focus Lisa's attention on the customers, making sure, however, that he delegates responsibility to Lisa for resuming their discussion later.

Stage 2: Preparing the Map

By midafternoon, during a lull in business, Lisa comes looking for Ric.

Lisa: Ric, you wanted to talk to me about that display?

Ric: Yes. Thanks for getting back to me. Do you have twenty to thirty minutes before things heat up again? (*Ric tunes in to Lisa and clarifies her availability for a meeting in which he plans to create a basic work activities map.*)

Lisa: Yeah, sure, this is the calm before the storm. Things will get busy about an hour from now.

Ric: Okay. Here's what I'd like to do. Can you help me with a little problem-solving? I want to show you how mapping works. We'll use the display as a starting point. Okay? (*Ric empowers Lisa and collaborates with her as a colleague, thereby strengthening the team.*)

Lisa: Sure . . .

Ric: We need to ask four basic questions: What are you doing? How much time does it take? What roadblocks get in your way? How much time do they take? We'll record the answers on a sheet of paper and then, separately, we'll ask another question: Based on what we know, what can we do to improve the situation? Let's start with the display. How long does it take you to put it together?

(Ric takes a blank sheet of paper and creates a Talent Mapping Data Collection Worksheet.)

Lisa: About an hour and a half, maybe two.

Ric: Is this a standard part of the job, or a roadblock?

Lisa: Let me think. We've been doing these for six months or so, as long as I've been here. Jill said that our vendors used to set up displays, but they stopped doing that.

Ric: Well, let's put it down as a To Do for the moment. How often do you put displays together? *(Ric begins to guide Lisa's analysis.)*

Talent Mapping Data Collection Worksheet	
What did we do? (To Do)	
Time it takes	
Roadblocks (problems that get in the way)	
Time consumed by roadblocks	

Lisa: Oh, a few. Maybe four, on average. But I get interrupted all the time. Maybe a half hour or more per display.

Ric: How much time does each take, on average?

Lisa: Two hours. Or less.

Ric: Well, that's interesting! So let's say three displays a week, totaling four and a half to six hours. Is that about right? *(Ric affirms Lisa's involvement and also her responsibility for the validity of the data by asking her to confirm the information she gave.)*

Leadership Talent Mapping Data Collection Worksheet	
What did we do? (To Do)	*Set up displays*
Time it takes	*1.5–2 hours each*
Roadblocks (problems that get in the way)	*Interruptions*
Time consumed by roadblocks	*Add 30–45 minutes to each display setup*

Lisa: Yes, but I'm a little shocked by the time. Maybe it's a little off. I'm working part-time now and that's a third of the time I spend here!

Ric: Don't worry about strict accuracy for now; we're just getting a general picture that's very helpful. Let's move to the next step and ask ourselves what we should do differently. Can you offer any general observations on what we've discovered before we move on to the really important question of what to do differently? *(Ric continues to increase Lisa's involvement in the process by delegating observation responsibilities to her.)*

193

Lisa: Well, I'm supposed to be getting paid for sales, but that's not what I'm doing—I'm a gofer, doing everything else or messing around with roadblocks. It's crazy. No wonder my commissions are down.

Ric: That's a breakthrough, Lisa! You can see how the way we organize our work can help harness our talent. Do you think we've learned enough to try to figure out what to do about it? *(Ric reinforces Lisa's observation and their mutual stake in solving the problem, and he sets the stage for a transition to actually finding solutions.)*

Lisa: Absolutely. I know we can fix this problem.

Ric: Terrific. Let's start to develop some answers to the question I mentioned earlier: Based on what we now know according to the map we've created, how can we improve your alignment on the job? Let's analyze our problem more closely.

Stage 3: Problem-Solving

During a relatively brief twenty-minute dialogue, we have seen Ric and Lisa move from discovery and definition of an alignment issue to a point where solutions can begin to emerge. Now Ric can apply the form on the following page for analyzing the results of the mapping process. Ric moves Lisa to the next stage of problem-solving by focusing their attention on what the data from the Talent Map can mean for achieving the one goal essential to their mutual success: customer sales and service.

Ric: Lisa, the question is, based on what we know now, how can we improve things? Let's ask, What must we do, and how do we increase the time spent doing that? Let's zero in right now on our main goal and try to come up with ways to achieve it. What's your number one Must Do priority? *(Ric draws Lisa's attention to her number one responsibility, thus clarifying her primary responsibilities.)*

Ric and Lisa's Problem Analysis and Solution Worksheet

TO-DO ACTIVITIES (GOALS)	TIME IT TAKES
1.	
2.	
3.	
4.	
5.	

ACTIVITIES THAT GET IN THE WAY (ROADBLOCKS)	TIME IT TAKES
1.	
2.	
3.	
4.	
5.	

SHOULD-DO ACTIVITIES (SOLUTIONS)	TIME IT TAKES
1.	
2.	
3.	
4.	
5.	

Lisa: That's very clear to me now: customer sales and anything related to it.

Ric: Okay. Let's put customer sales down as the number one To Do. How can *you* increase the time you spend on it?

Lisa: Well, frankly, by dropping whatever else could interfere and serving the customer first. That makes customer service my main To Do and makes setting up displays a big roadblock. Wow!

Ric: Bingo! I think you have a very clear sense of your priorities. There's only one reason we're really here. Anything that gets in the way of customer service has got to be moved out of the way, streamlined, or eliminated. Right? *(Ric applauds Lisa's insight, reinforcing its value, her role, and his expectations of her. He then takes her to the next stage, which includes a thorough analysis of the problem and sharing of the responsibility for solutions.)*

Lisa: Absolutely.

Ric: Good. Well, let's follow through and identify our roadblocks and what we should do to overcome them. Let's make sure we assign clear responsibility for improvement. We're all in this together. After we're done, I'll meet with the rest of the team individually as well. Okay, let's put our analysis together. *(Ric explains how the Leadership Talent Mapping process is central to overall team effectiveness, orienting Lisa toward her individual responsibility for service as well as to her connection to the whole team. They complete the Problem Analysis and Solution Worksheet and produce a practical plan for action.)*

196

Ric: Well, Lisa, I think we've made a good start on addressing this problem. It looks to me like we've got a problem-solving plan we can put into action right now. Everyone should benefit. If we spend 75 to 80 percent of our work week with customers, the quality of our service and our productivity should rise a solid 18 percent.

Lisa: One thing's for sure, I've got a better handle on what my priorities need to be to do a better job.

Ric: That's great! Perhaps we should go through this exercise more regularly. How about we meet next week for fifteen to twenty minutes to review our solution to this problem and tackle another one? Can you think of any other time wasters that get in your way?

Lisa: Yeah. That new PC network. It's full of bugs.

Ric and Lisa's Problem Analysis and Solution Worksheet	
TO-DO ACTIVITIES (GOALS)	TIME IT TAKES
1. Customer sales	14 hours of an 18-hour work week
ACTIVITIES THAT GET IN THE WAY (ROADBLOCKS)	TIME IT TAKES
1. Setting up displays	6 hours a week
SHOULD-DO ACTIVITIES (SOLUTIONS)	TIME IT TAKES
1. All salespeople ask vendors to set up displays	.5 hour
2. Ric: Hire temporary help to set up displays if necessary	20 minutes (+ wage)
3. Ric arrange: Rotate displays that have been set up in other stores in the chain	1.5 hours for the setup of one display

Ric: Okay. Let's put that on our agenda. Hey, we've got customers coming in. Let's get going! (*Ric has moved Lisa through the process to a point where she can take action to solve a problem. He also clarifies his expectations for follow-up and suggests that Leadership Talent Mapping become a more conscious, continuing part of their work life.*)

Case #2: Team Leadership Talent Mapping

Sarah Eddins, vice president of patient care for the oncology center at one of America's leading medical centers, used Leadership Talent Mapping to improve her team's patient care delivery. "To what extent do we put the 'right people in the right place for the right amount of time to deliver quality and cost-effective care?' It has become even more crucial in light of recent operational downsizing." Sarah convenes a team problem-solving meeting devoted to identifying and solving this serious service and financial problem.

The workers most affected by this issue are the registered nurses (RNs), whose hourly wage is 50 percent higher than practical nurses' wages, and 100 percent higher than nurse assistants' (NAs) and secretaries' wages. How can her leadership team better utilize nursing talent to improve care while addressing the pressing cost issues that threaten the institution's future? Sarah starts the meeting with Jim, Melissa, and Paul by focusing everyone on that goal.

Sarah: Good morning. Well, as we all know, the subject today is how to realign our unit so the right person is in the—

Jim, Melissa, and Paul (in unison): —right place at the right time and cost for quality.

Sarah: You're clairvoyant! We'll need to remember that as we tackle this issue. I've assembled all the input we gathered earlier about the problem. We know what everyone is doing. We'll use that map to help us make important redesign decisions. But before handing out the data, I'd like to ask each of you to help me with a special exercise. It involves two parts. First, I'd like us to describe the profile of a typical patient on our unit, and his or her chief concerns. Then second, I want us to look at the work through that patient's eyes. Jim, you've been working with patient satisfaction and profile data. Describe a patient for us. (*Sarah demonstrates deep commitment to the mission and her team by framing the problem in the context of their shared responsibility to the customer—the patient.*)

Jim: Okay. I've been reading our patients' comments, so I think I can give you a patient's point of view. Let's say I'm a fifty-four-year-old man just admitted to this unit with prostate cancer. I'm pretty nervous about what type of treatment I'm going to receive, but I don't want to panic. My concerns are: Can anyone tell me what's going on and what my options are? How are the surgical and chemotherapy procedures carried out? What are the chances that treatment will be successful? I'm probably also worried because my assessment interview was done by a female resident physician half my age and I've had to put up with interminable delays for every aspect of my treatment so far, which causes me a lot of stress.

Paul: Jim, I feel stressed just hearing you put those perceptions together. Is that what our patients are feeling?

Sarah: Yes, I've read their evaluations, too. Jim paints a realistic picture. Let's take his example and ask ourselves this: If we were that male patient and making decisions here, what work would take highest priority? How do we achieve our goal—our Must Do—of delivering the highest-quality care despite recent and potential financial difficulties? I'll keep track of the comments on the Problem Analysis and Solution Worksheet. (*Sarah focuses the team on the core issue, involving everyone and building shared responsibility.*)

Paul: Well, I'd put patient assessment, education, and counseling at the top of the list.

Melissa: I agree with Paul, but I'd add giving medication, especially chemotherapy.

Paul: You'd better note physician support, too. And if we're going to think of this from a patient's perspective, we have to add such nitty-gritty things as room cleanliness, staff courtesy, and promptness.

Sarah: Excellent! Anything else? (*Sarah leads the team through an intensive ten-minute problem analysis session.*) Now, before going any further, let's take a look at the data we compiled that shows us what everybody is actually doing. Let me call your attention to one fact. Our RNs reported that they are spending less than 25 percent of their time on the Should Do(s) you just identified. I just circled them. The data also showed that RNs spent a considerable amount of time on such activities as general clerical duties, feeding, getting supplies, housekeeping, toileting, linen change, transportation, and bathing, as well as on more appropriate activities such as patient assessment, medication, patient counseling and education, and physician support. All in all, their jobs are complex—they reported forty-four activities—and stressful. With this data and our Must Do(s) in mind, what are your observations? What are the roadblocks, the things that get in the way? (*Sarah hands out the report that compares the percentage of time nurses spend on the top fifteen time-consuming activities in their job with the percentage of time others spend doing the same work.*)

Melissa: Well, I know I should say I'm shocked, but I'm really not surprised. We have a virtual role reversal of responsibilities. The nurses spend too much time on clerical and other activities that shouldn't be a part of their job. And I'm afraid that this situation exists all over the place, not just here in oncology.

Paul: Exactly right. We have our most expensive people, our RNs, doing the support work.

Jim: But remember, I'm the patient. I still want someone to talk to me about my condition and to make sure my linen's clean. I say we need to get our nurses refocused by redistributing and eliminating unnecessary work, but making sure there's qualified staff available to provide good support.

Sarah: Okay. I agree, and I'd like to ask you one more set of questions. (*Having moved the team to a stage of high involvement and empowerment, Sarah decides to move toward solutions.*)

Paul: Oh no. I don't know if I can take it!

Sarah: Relax, Paul. These are very direct and logical. I'd like to propose that we consider the almost unthinkable—namely, reducing the number of our RN staff to accomplish two things: first, to free some dollars to get more support staff. This way we can make sure that the patients' linen is always clean, that meals are served while they're still hot, and that someone always answers the call bell. We can hire several nursing assistants if we cut only a few RN positions. Second, getting this support staff will allow us to focus more of the remaining RNs' time on the Must Do patient care work that only they are qualified to do. As you'll notice, between the percentages of time RNs are spending on support work and other things, well over 40 percent of their time and our labor dollars are wasted. They're not doing nurses' work, but other work. Making it possible for nurses to do the work they're supposed to be doing benefits everybody, especially the patients. (*Sarah pushes forward to the next and most difficult level of the problem—cost reduction.*)

Paul: Hold on, Sarah, now we're treading on sacred territory. How do you justify the move?

Sarah: With the data. And this data came from our staff, who have told us that RNs' jobs are so fragmented that they're not focused on core responsibilities, which means that the *quality is threatened.*

And this is just as relevant: The quality of life for RNs is suffering because of *high stress* due to the lack of focus on patient care and the fact that their job is so complex by comparison with others.

Melissa: It's true. The data does justify those conclusions.

Jim: And I think the staff already understands the situation as well. After all, they're the ones who gave us this data.

Sarah: That's what I've been thinking. In order to address patients' concerns as Jim outlined them for us, and the work design problems our data has revealed, we have to take some definite steps, like the Should Do(s) we've ended up with on our Problem Analysis and Solution Worksheet. Take a look: Does it sum things up and point us to a solution? *(Sarah brings the team back to its original goal of finding solutions for delivering quality care.)*

Jim: It's tough, but accurate. Unless we get our nurses refocused, patient care will suffer.

Melissa: And the cost issue really makes things clear. We're paying top dollar for our nurses to do the wrong work.

Paul: Yeah. But there are going to be some really skeptical people out there who are not going to like these results.

Sarah: I agree with all of you. We do have to get our nurses focused and use our money more responsibly. And yes, Paul, there is skepticism, which I would like to suggest we meet head-on. We'll have to conduct problem-solving sessions like this one for our physicians and staff in order to involve them in the process. Paul, which sessions do you think should come first?

(Sarah has used the problem-solving process to research the issue and suggest a solution she has been mulling over. However, she knows that

her team must address several practical issues before implementation, including the issue of resistance, which Paul represents. She pulls Paul in by turning his natural skepticism to good use. To do this, she uses the technique of asking Paul to react to some options rather than giving him open-ended questions that might cause him further anxiety and stimulate an oppositional response.)

Paul: Either or both, as soon as we've got our act together. This is too important to wait any longer. In fact, I'd use this same exercise you used with us. When they look at this through the eyes of the patient, it makes things much more clear.

Sarah: Thanks, I agree. Let's figure out how we can go about it.

Sarah's Problem Analysis and Solution Worksheet for Jim's Case Study
TO DO ACTIVITIES (GOALS)
1. Deliver even better service despite operational downsizing
ACTIVITIES THAT GET IN THE WAY (ROADBLOCKS)
1. Reversal of responsibilities for the RN *2. RN role doing clerical work and getting supplies* *3. Nurses not focused on their real job*
SHOULD DO ACTIVITIES (SOLUTIONS)
1. Refocus nurses on patient assessment, patient education, patient counseling, giving medications (chemotherapy), physician support
2. Redistribute support work from nurses to others, and . . .
3. Consider reducing the number of RNs to hire more support staff

Sarah spends another ten minutes with the team, planning the next steps. She knows it's vitally important to conclude every problem-solving session by establishing a practical course of action. Like Ric and Lisa, she gathered data, used the data to define the problem, and then she and her team developed potential solutions using the Problem Analysis and Solution Worksheet.

Case #3: Organizational Leadership Talent Mapping

Dennis Chow, chair and CEO of the Exsular Group, oversees a rapidly expanding southeastern lighting and electronics distribution company. As he tells the story, "We had been on a three-year tear; profits were way up. But, the sudden resignations of two of our leading execs and several unexpected new location startup glitches gave me the sense we were headed off a cliff. Something was significantly amiss, and I wasn't going to wait for disaster to hit before acting. That's when I called Wayne and he told me about Leadership Talent Mapping."

"I was glad Dennis responded to the signals," said Wayne Randall, vice chair and largest shareholder. "When we lost our senior VP for new operations, along with our comptroller, the signals were too clear to avoid. This company has only one true resource, its talent. More than technology or market conditions, it's talent burnout and misalignment that will do us in. I told Dennis about Leadership Talent Mapping, which I learned about from my friend, Warren Brueggeman from GE. We needed to understand what was happening, but we needed to make sure we were recommitting and redesigning as we did so. Places like Exsular can be both tremendously resilient and fragile at the same time. We can handle pretty much anything as long as we have our key people."

Since Dennis always valued Wayne's insights, he immediately launched a leadership mapping effort involving Exsular's top seventy-eight managers and executives. They used a special leadership mapping technique that incorporated a leadership work activities dictionary developed as part of the Talent IQ research project. Rather than just asking leaders what they were doing, this dictionary *defined* the core activities typically constituting a leader's work. This dictionary greatly accelerated the process of getting answers to the questions, "What do you do and how much time does it take?" and "What gets in your way and how much time does it take?" In addition to the dictionary, the Talent IQ research provided a map of the time top-performing leaders spend on specific activities. This gave Dennis and his team a way to benchmark their performance and diagnose particular issues that were undermining the performance of the leadership team and, thus, the corporation.

I helped Dennis and five of the most respected leaders in the company to carry out the interviewing process. They first went through individual mapping interviews with me to gain personal insight into the mapping interview experience. Then, they attended special training seminars to prepare for other issues that might arise during the process. When they had completed this training, they traveled to locations throughout the Southeast to carry out the interviews. Following the interviews, they aggregated the data into a leadership Talent Map for the Exsular group.

Leadership Talent Map for the Exsular Group			
Leadership Activity	Leadership Benchmark	Exsular Leadership Yr. 1 Avg. Score	Exsular Leadership Yr. 2 Avg. Score
Problem-Solving	52	31	44
Selection Evaluation Conflict Management Negotiation Communication	30	16	25
Nonproductive • Roadblocks • Maintenance	18	53	31

The left column of the map lists the general activities assessed during interviews, including nonproductive roadblocks (such time-wasting work experiences as phone and personal interruptions, duplicating work that should have been or was completed by others, and tracking down information that was not provided as promised or required). Nonproductive maintenance addressed the simple life necessities of any job (coffee and bathroom breaks, the logistics of office and computer setup, and so on).

The next column indicates the Talent IQ benchmarks, while the next two compare Exsular's results to the benchmarks. (The benchmark performance study included more than 3,000 high-performing leaders.) After determining the average score for year one, the executives identified certain "should do" items aimed at improving their score. The top three items for the group were (1) to regain focus on the core mission; (2) to establish clear priorities for work; and (3) to re-engage associates at all levels in an examination of how to improve performance. With the results of the Leadership Map and these answers in mind, the Exsular leaders embarked on a performance improvement program that resulted in better scores for year two. "The overall Leadership Talent Map documented a reality none of us wanted to see," noted Dennis. "I guess we all had a sense that we had lost our bearings, but the threat was far more acute than I had thought. The lack of frontline problem-solving was most glaring because it told me we were not 'there' for either our associates or customers. When I flippantly asked where we were, I was brought up short by an answer that hit too close to home—*out to lunch*. Emmett was my Mapping coach, and he asked me how much time I was spending in direct involvement with company strategy and operations as compared to external meetings with bankers, investors, and philanthropy. The answer was about 30 percent to 70 percent on what my team members called 'lunch.' No wonder we were unfocused. It all started with me."

Gina Palmeri, COO of Exsular, observed, "We all had to take a deep breath and get into the specifics. When we broke the data into greater detail, we realized that the high percentage of nonproductive work was due to a lack of purpose and discipline in the way we used the only real raw material we have—time. We just frittered it away. Adopting the Team Problem-Solving process from the HP model helped. Plus, we got very specific about charging ourselves and leaders at all levels to lead from the frontlines, not the office. We also realized that the lack of time invested in the core functional areas explained the rebelliousness and turnover we were experiencing. When we shifted the emphasis to coaching, the vast majority of conflict and evaluation headaches went away, and turnover went down like a rock."

"The bottom line," concluded Dennis, "was that once we got ourselves realigned and focused, the quality and financial bottom line went from so-so to fantastic. Within twelve months the future we were planning for transformed from one of anxiety to one of real promise. Our year two Map shows how we are progressing. Most important, it showed all of us, me especially, that the issue wasn't our intrinsic ability. We could have fired everyone, hired all new people, and still had the same problem. We weren't translating our potential into talent that mattered. We're getting there now."

"From the board's point of view," observed Wayne, "we needed to see that the company had and would continue to have the leadership talent it needed. In addition to a very thorough inventory of our present and future leadership needs, and a blueprint to meet them, a key part of the Leadership Talent Mapping process involved meetings with groups of leaders at different levels that Dennis set up so that we could see for ourselves how leaders felt about the future. It was involvement in the process that told them we were serious about this company's, and, thus, their future. They told us in no uncertain terms that continuously updating and renewing that plan was more important than anything else we could do to make sure we had what it would take to sustain success."

The ultimate issue in talent management is this: "Will the talent you need be in the right place at the right time to fulfill the mission?" Every leader must challenge talented people to take stock of how they spend the most finite of resources—time.

The Talent IQ research drove home this most basic point and reminded us of this timeless issue. Regardless of how noisy and chaotic the world may become, everyone who seeks to make a difference needs to prepare a Leadership Talent Map to guide them to achievement.

The Talent Imperative

IT MAY SEEM AN all-too-obvious conclusion, but the results of our Talent IQ research project underscored the necessity for talented leaders to surround themselves with talented people. No individual, team, or organization ever accomplishes anything without talent and the knowledge—the Talent IQ—that helps identify, develop, and retain the people who provide the creativity, quality, and profits that propel organizational achievement.

The commitment to developing talent distinguishes high-achieving organizations from their average and low-performing counterparts. The Talent IQ research revealed that, revenue dollar for dollar, the operational agenda of top-performing organizations included 200 percent more activity aimed at talent development than did the agendas of average-performing organizations, and well over 400 percent more than the poorly performing ones. We measured performance in terms of a combined score of profitability, customer satisfaction, employee turnover, and commitment over the last three years of the study. Fifteen percent of the 983 organizations ranked high, 65 percent average, and 15 percent poor.

What comprised "talent-building activities?" Such activities fell into five areas:

- *First,* the executive team participated in regularly scheduled retreats and seminars that focused on the effective development and alignment of talent.
- *Second,* key individuals received coaching to harness their individual talents more effectively in their present roles while preparing them for future ones.
- *Third,* mid-level and frontline managers received regular instruction in talent management. One of the most creative techniques involved the use of a regularly scheduled leadership forum that included presentations designed by both external authorities and internal leaders to address issues identified in confidential leadership needs surveys.
- *Fourth,* top-performing organizations evaluated performance in terms of mission focus on the individual, team, and organization-wide levels. They translated their commitment to service into action that honored and rewarded those who contributed the most to the central purpose for the organization's existence.
- *Fifth,* top performers created "talent images" of the alignment and distribution of their most talented people. As the study progressed, this became a more formal and routine process driven by an open, transparent collaboration explicitly designed to help individuals *and* the organization focus their talents more effectively for both present achievement and future success.

As our work proceeded, we collected a number of specific best practices regarding these five areas of talent development. You may contact us if you would like to receive further information about the specific reports we have written about the practices. E-mail us at *ECMurphy@ECMurphyWalsh.com.*

This book began and continues as an unending journey, one that keeps taking us farther and farther across the globe. Yet, as we travel, we keep making the same humbling and amazing discovery: All people share similar aspirations and best practices.

That should come as no surprise, of course. Joseph Campbell, the great scholar of mythology, noted that all people share a universal concept of what is best in human behavior. In a discussion of his landmark book, *The Hero with a Thousand Faces*, he noted, "We all share a universal bond with the heroic. From Buddha to Christ to Moses and Mohammed, our search for what is divine and true is essentially the same. From time to time, we are saved by the quests of great heroes who search for answers to our most vexing troubles and, upon finding them, return to share them with us and guide us from one state of existence to a new and better one. These heroes are our hope and redemption."

Heroes fulfill their talent potential; true talent acts heroically. That's the ultimate conclusion. The search for such heroes goes on today. We can increase the possibility of the heroic by increasing our Talent IQ, the knowledge and skills required to identify, develop, and retain those who can give us a glimpse of what is the true standard.

Bibliography

The following have been useful resources in shaping the results of the Talent IQ research for the body of the book.

Bellah, Robert, et al. *Habits of the Heart.* Berkeley: University of California Press, 1996.

Bloom, Harold. *Where Shall Wisdom Be Found?* New York: Riverhead, 2004.

Darby, David, and Kevin Walsh. *Neuropsychology.* New York: Elsevier Health Sciences, 2005.

Fallows, James. *More Like Us.* New York: Houghton Mifflin, 1990.

Gardner, Howard. *Leading Minds.* New York: Basic Books, 1995.

Groopman, Jerome. *The Anatomy of Hope.* New York: Random House, 2004.

Halberstam, Michael. *The Wanting of Levine.* New York: Penguin, 1979.

Kahneman, Daniel, and Amos Tversky, eds. *Choices, Values and Frames.* Cambridge: Cambridge University Press, 2000.

Labovitz, George, and Victor Rosansky. *The Power of Alignment.* New York: Wiley, 1997.

Lezak, Muriel D., et al. *Neuropsychological Assessment.* Oxford; New York: Oxford University Press, 2004.

McClelland, David. *The Achievement Motive.* New York: Irvington, 1992.

———. *The Achieving Society.* New York: Macmillan, 1985.

Moore, Geoffrey A. *Living on the Fault Line.* New York: HarperBusiness, 2002.

Murphy, Emmett. *The New Murphy's Law.* Worcester, MA: Chandler House Press, 1998.

———. *Leadership IQ.* New York: Prentice Hall, 1996.

———. *Forging the Heroic Organization.* Englewood Cliffs, NJ: Prentice Hall, 1994.

———. *The Genius of Sitting Bull.* Englewood Cliffs, NJ: Prentice Hall, 1993.

Murphy, Emmett, and Grant B. Walsh. "Talent IQ: A Comprehensive Study of Talent Management Practices in the Global Economy." Unpublished manuscript, EC Murphy Walsh, New York, 2007.

Murphy, Emmett, and Joseph Turner. *Practical Management on Psychiatric Units.* Chicago: Wellington Press, 1997.

Murphy, Emmett, and Mark Murphy. *Leadership at the Edge of Chaos.* Paramus, NJ: Prentice Hall, 2002.

———. "Cutting Healthcare Costs through Work Force Reductions." *Healthcare Financial Management*, July 1996.

Ratey, John J. *A User's Guide to the Brain*. New York: Vintage, 2001.

Santoro, Joseph, and Ronald Jay Cohen. *The Angry Heart*. New York: New Harbinger, 1997.

Seligman, Martin E. *Learned Optimism*. New York: Knopf, 2006.

———. *Authentic Happiness*. New York: Free Press, 2002.

Terkel, Studs. *Working*. New York: New Press, 1997.

Watson, Peter. *The Modern Mind*. New York: Perennial, 2000.

The following works provide insight into the specific characteristics of achievement demonstrated by TalentLeaders.

Achievement

Atkinson, John. *Personality, Motivation, and Achievement*. New York: Wiley, 1978.

Atkinson, John, and Norman T. Feather, eds. *Theory of Achievement Motivation*. Huntington, NY: R. E. Krieger, 1974.

McClelland, David. *The Achievement Motive*. New York: Irvington, 1992.

———. *Human Motivation*. Cambridge University Press, 1987.

———. *The Achieving Society*. New York: Macmillan, 1985.

215

Murray, Henry. *Thematic Apperception Test Manual.* Cambridge, MA: Harvard University Press, 1943.

Pragmatism

Dewey, John. 1938. *Logic: The Theory of Inquiry.* In *John Dewey, The Later Works, 1925–1953,* Volume 12: 1938, edited by Jo Ann Boydston and Kathleen Poulos, 1–527. Carbondale and Edwardsville, IL: Southern Illinois University Press, 1986.

James, William. 1902. "Pragmatic and Pragmatism." In J. M. Baldwin, *Dictionary of Philosophy and Psychology,* vol. 2. New York: Macmillan. Reprinted, CP 5.2 in C. S. Peirce, *Collected Papers.*

Peirce, C. S. *The Essential Peirce: Selected Philosophical Writings, Volume 1 (1867–1893),* edited by Nathan Houser and Christian Kloesel. Bloomington and Indianapolis, IN: Indiana University Press, 1992.

Humility

Furey, Robert J. *So I'm Not Perfect: A Psychology of Humility.* Staten Island, NY: Alba House, 1990.

Grenberg, Jeanine. *Kant and the Ethics of Humility.* New York: Cambridge University Press, 2005.

Mack, Wayne, and Joshua Mack. *Humility: The Forgotten Virtue.* Phillipsburg, NJ: P&R Publishing, 2005.

Mahaney, C. J. *Humility: True Greatness.* Gaithersburg, MD: Sovereign Grace Ministries, 2005.

Murray, Andrew. *Humility.* Minneapolis: Bethany House Publishers, 2004.

Neuschel, Robert P. *The Servant Leader.* Evanston, IL: Northwestern University Press, 2005.

Wilke, Lori. *Requirements for Greatness: Justice, Mercy and Humility.* Shippensburg, PA: Destiny Image Publishers, 1996.

Service

Axelrod, Robert. *The Complexity of Cooperation.* Princeton, NJ: Princeton University Press, 1997.

————. *The Evolution of Cooperation.* New York: Basic Books, 1984.

————, ed. *Structure of Decision.* Princeton, NJ: Princeton University Press, 1976.

Axelrod, Robert, and Douglas Dion. "The Further Evolution of Cooperation." *Science* 242 (9 December 1988): 1385–1390.

Axelrod, Robert, and Michael D. Cohen. *Harnessing Complexity.* New York: Free Press, 2001.

Campbell, Joseph. *The Hero with a Thousand Faces.* Princeton, NJ: Princeton University Press, 1972.

Gintis, Herbert (ed.), et al. *Moral Sentiments and Material Interests.* Cambridge, MA: MIT Press, 2005.

Murphy, Emmett C. *Reciprocity and Partnership: The Science Behind the Golden Rule and Its Implications for Leadership.* Presentation, Annual Conference of the American Hospital Association, August 2002.

Neuschel, Robert P. *The Servant Leader.* Evanston, IL: Northwestern University Press, 2005.

Osborne, Martin J. *An Introduction to Game Theory.* New York: Oxford University Press, 2003.

Commitment

Hesselbein, Frances, and Paul M. Cohen, eds. *Leader to Leader.* San Francisco: Jossey-Bass, 1999.

Maddi, Salvatore R. *Personality Theories.* Long Grove, IL: Waveland Press, 1996.

———, ed. *Perspectives on Personality.* Boston: Little, Brown, 1971.

Maddi, Salvatore R., and Deborah M. Khoshaba. *Resilience at Work.* New York: AMACOM, 2005.

———. *Hardy Executive.* New York: McGraw-Hill, 1984.

O'Malley, Michael. *Creating Commitment.* New York: Wiley, 2000.

Hope

Murray, Bob, and Alicia Fortinberry. *Creating Optimism.* New York: McGraw-Hill, 2005.

———. *Raising an Optimistic Child.* New York: McGraw-Hill, 2005.

Seligman, Martin. *Learned Optimism.* New York: Knopf, 2006.

———. *Authentic Happiness*. New York: Free Press, 2004.

———. *The Optimistic Child*. New York: HarperPerennial, 1996.

———. *What You Can Change . . . and What You Can't*. New York: Random House, 1995.

Responsibility

Gallo, Eileen, and Jon Gallo. *Silver Spoon Kids: How Successful Parents Raise Responsible Children*. New York: McGraw-Hill, 2001.

Glasser, William. *Choice Theory*. New York: HarperCollins, 1999.

———. *The Quality School*. New York: HarperPerennial, 1998.

———. *Reality Therapy*. New York: HarperCollins, 1989.

Miller, John. *Flipping the Switch: Unleash the Power of Personal Accountability Using the QBQ!* New York: Penguin, 2005.

———. *QBQ! The Question Behind the Question: Practicing Personal Accountability in Work and in Life*. New York: Penguin, 2004.

Wubbolding, Robert E. *Using Reality Therapy*. Foreword by William Glasser. New York: Perennial Library, 1988.

The Talent IQ Assessment

WE HAVE DESIGNED the Talent IQ (TIQ) Assessment to help you determine your present levels of accomplishment with respect to the principles and skills we have presented in this book.

The assessment employs scenarios based on the scripts that TalentLeaders use every day. Our TalentLeader research revealed that these scripts and the effective strategies and tools they employ often defy intuition and conventional logic. In other words, they often challenge traditional approaches. Sometimes the scripts differ only subtly from conventional practice, but even slight differences can greatly influence outcomes.

As you apply the assessment, look for these slight but significant differences as well as for more dramatic ones. Following the assessment, you will find a list of the chapters in this book in which specific skills appear. Once you identify specific areas for improvement revealed by the TIQ Assessment, you may want to consult the chapters that focus on those skills.

The Talent IQ Assessment

Directions: The TIQ Assessment presents possible solutions to specific scenarios. Read each scenario and *circle one of the three choices offered.* After completing the assessment, compare your answers to the Answer Key provided at the end of the assessment. The key will reveal your present overall Talent IQ and help you target areas for improvement.

Consult the Development Guide at the end of this appendix to find specific sections of the book that explain the logic behind the best choice.

1. In order to exert your influence as a leader, you must first:
   A. Rely on your own personal achievement.
   B. Build a community of achievers.
   C. Rely on others' achievements.

2. A good leader:
   A. Relies on personal achievements to get ahead.
   B. Relies on who they know to get ahead.
   C. Relies on the power they wield to get ahead.

3. As a new manager for the marketing department of a computer software company, you must make an important decision affecting the department. Not yet completely familiar with the department, you:
   A. Tell your superiors that you don't feel comfortable making a decision at this time because you do not know the department well enough. It's better to admit that you can't handle a situation than to make a bad decision that will affect the whole department.
   B. Use the information you do possess to make the most informed decision possible; you don't want your superiors, or the members of your department, to think you are incapable of handling your new position.

C. Admit that you don't know enough about the department to make the best decision, and ask for information from the person or people with the most experience in the department. This will allow you to make an informed decision.

4. In a culture of achievement, which of the following is/are true?
   A. The most outstanding performer threatens the majority who need improvement.
   B. The least outstanding performer serves as an anchor of negativity and contempt and drags down everyone else.
   C. The most outstanding performer exerts no influence on the majority who need improvement.

5. Before interviewing candidates for a position, you must first and foremost:
   A. Identify the technical skills necessary to excel in that position.
   B. Identify how you believe a successful person in that position should act.
   C. Rely on the recommendations and praise or criticism of the candidate's former superiors and colleagues.

6. When conducting an initial hiring interview, ask first:
   A. "Can you walk me through your work history, starting with the first job you ever held?"
   B. "Can you tell me about your greatest professional accomplishment?"
   C. "Can you tell me what you are looking for in your next position?"

7. When an employee of yours fails to perform up to standard, you should:
   A. Arrange to meet with the employee to confide that you feel it's time for him to move on to a new position.
   B. Arrange to meet with the employee and suggest it's time he separated from the company.
   C. Arrange to meet with the employee to discuss his accomplishments in his current position, and ask the person to share his feelings about that.

8. Choose the most accurate statement about coaching:
   A. Coaching should be undertaken as a career development exercise to help achievers improve their focus on mission-critical work and skill sets.
   B. Coaching should be undertaken over time to allow achievers to learn "on the job" by trial and error and gain real-world experience with the guidance of a professional.
   C. Most importantly, coaching should be undertaken in the context of a real and definable performance need.

9. An effective Problem-Solving Inventory should reveal:
   A. How an individual approaches a problem or decision.
   B. The right way to solve a problem.
   C. The consequences of poor solutions.

10. When you have selected an individual for coaching, you should first:
    A. Interview her to give her a chance to speak to her accomplishments and ask if she wishes to participate in coaching.
    B. Meet with her to tell her that since she needs to demonstrate improvements in certain areas of work, you have selected her for coaching.
    C. Meet with her to tell her that she needs coaching, whether she realizes it or not.

Use the following scenario to answer questions 11–13:

You manage a major department at a large computer software company. Dave, a new software developer who has shown great skill as a creative problem-solver, has been struggling to solve a particularly vexing problem for weeks. You begin to notice that he has become withdrawn, less engaged, and self-absorbed. He also appears angry and has become increasingly tense around his colleagues, including you.

11. Dave most likely behaves this way because:
    A. He has been offered a higher position at another company.
    B. He has come up with a solution to the problem but is withholding it.
    C. Another member of the staff has been picking on Dave for his inability to solve the problem, and Dave has become increasingly insecure, and is overcompensating by acting arrogantly.

12. If Dave's arrogant attitude persists, he will probably:
    A. Become frozen with anxiety, like a deer in headlights, and become unable to perform his job.
    B. Start displaying martyr-like behavior, such as blaming others for his shortcomings.
    C. Resort to bullying behavior, verbally abusing other employees and attacking the quality of their work.

13. If his behavior is left unchecked, Dave will:
    A. Become increasingly withdrawn, until he eventually resigns.
    B. Become increasingly hostile, exploiting the anxiety and fear of others to get ahead.
    C. Become increasingly frustrated and begin to spread gossip about his coworkers to deflect attention from his shortcomings.

Use the following scenario to answer questions 14–17:

As the sales manager for an appliance company, you have just learned that your company will be focusing on the sale of its WashRight washing machine via a new initiative involving e-mail marketing. Your sales department typically meets face-to-face with its client base to make sales, so you know that this may cause concern among certain employees. You prepare a presentation and call a department meeting.

14. In order for your message to reach everyone in your audience, you should begin your comments with:

    A. "The data shows that we should focus on the sale of our WashRight washing machine using e-mail marketing, which Mark's team will implement. I understand this may make us uncomfortable initially, but it will help us serve our customers better."

    B. "The data shows that we should focus on the sale of our WashRight washing machine using e-mail marketing. I'm sure you'll all agree that this is an exciting new initiative that we will all work hard to make a success."

    C. "The data shows that we should focus on the sale of our WashRight washing machine using e-mail marketing, which will be easier than our usual method of meeting face-to-face with our customers."

15. During this meeting, Sylvia resists change, interrupting you to question preparations to accommodate the e-mail marketing initiative. You should address her concerns by first saying:

   A. "I assure you, Sylvia, we've got everything under control. At this stage in the game, the details aren't important."

   B. "Sylvia, I understand you're concerned because we've never used e-mail marketing before and we haven't set up a procedure for it yet; however, our research results show us that this is what we need to do in order to fulfill our mission."

   C. "I understand that you're concerned, Sylvia; however, I assure you that once everything's in place, you'll really love the e-mail marketing campaign."

16. Not satisfied with your response, Sylvia again disrupts the meeting by repeatedly airing her concerns. You respond to her by saying:

   A. "Sylvia, as soon as I receive more information regarding this initiative, I assure you I will contact you immediately because I understand your great concern."

   B. "Sylvia, it appears that I am not getting my message across clearly. I'll ask another manager to discuss this with you privately after the meeting."

   C. "Sylvia, it appears that you do not understand my message. You're disrupting our goals. You and I will meet privately to talk about this issue. We simply cannot continue in this fashion."

17. Sylvia's interruptions represent:

   A. Resistance

   B. Attenuation

   C. Crosstalk

Use the following scenario to answer questions 18 and 19:
You are the store manager of a large retail operation. Corporate has just informed you of a new initiative it will roll out within the month involving a Customer Benefits Card. For a cost of $20.00 a year, customers can present their card at the register and get 10 percent off every purchase they make in the store. You decide to hold individual meetings with your department managers to explain this initiative.

18. You first approach Enrique, the head cashier, who is highly intuitive. In order to get Enrique excited about the initiative, you tell him:
    A. "Your team will be especially involved with this initiative because they will be in charge of explaining and selling the Customer Benefits Card to each customer at the registers."
    B. "Our research shows that stores with Customer Benefits Cards achieve a higher rate of customer loyalty than stores without one."
    C. "This new opportunity will help increase our customer loyalty and attract customers away from our competitors' stores."

19. Next you approach Cindy, manager of the housewares department, who is highly rational. In order to get Cindy excited about the new initiative, you tell her:
    A. "Your team will be involved with this initiative because they will be in charge of explaining the Customer Benefits Card to each customer they help."
    B. "Our research shows that stores with Customer Benefits Cards achieve a higher rate of customer loyalty than stores without one."
    C. "This exciting new opportunity will increase our customer loyalty and divert customers from our competitors' stores."

20. When you are conducting an organization-wide evaluation, you should:
    A. Keep the results of the evaluation private.
    B. Only measure what you're willing to share.
    C. Keep some of the results private, revealing only selected information to selected individuals.

21. Conducting an evaluation interview for one of your employees, Sandra, you can best ensure her commitment to make specific improvements by:
    A. Suggesting that both you and Sandra fill out an evaluation form rating her performance.
    B. Focusing on your own evaluation of her performance.
    C. Encouraging Sandra to restrict discussion to her own performance evaluation.

22. The purpose of employee evaluation is:
    A. To suggest improvements to the employee.
    B. To keep employees "on their toes" and make sure they follow through with their work requirements.
    C. To discuss an employee's strengths, as well as to suggest areas he or she might improve.

Use the following scenario to answer questions 23–25:
You are the team leader for a group mobilized to address the challenge of increasing customer service satisfaction at your manufacturing company.

23. Before you do anything else, you should:
    A. Perform a cost-benefit analysis.
    B. Identify your problem-solving style and that of each of your team members.
    C. Create a plan that addresses the questions, "Who will do what, by when, and with what resources?"

24. Immediately after your team has accepted the challenge:
    A. It should first brainstorm the situation in an effort to develop a broad understanding of the factors that have contributed to the problem.
    B. It should come up with "problem statements" that simplify the challenge as much as possible.
    C. It should start developing solutions to the problem.

25. After your team has selected the most viable solutions to the challenge and proposes a plan to carry them out, you should:
    A. Conduct a cost-benefit analysis during implementation to see whether or not the plan is falling below, meeting, or exceeding expectations.
    B. Perform a cost-benefit analysis after implementation of the plan to see if it fell below, met, or exceeded expectations.
    C. Complete a cost-benefit analysis before seeking authorization of your plan in order to see if it will fall below, meet, or exceed expectations.

26. When you bring two or more employees together to discuss a conflict, you should:
    A. Direct the flow of discussion and draw very specific information from each participant.
    B. Remain hands-off, just making sure the meeting doesn't get too far out of control.
    C. Tell participants that "this is the way it's going to be."

27. If you bring two or more employees together to discuss a conflict and you cannot initially help them reach a consensus, you should:
    A. Adjourn the meeting for a day or two.
    B. Keep the meeting going until they reach consensus.
    C. Adjourn the meeting and explore the situation further with each one.

28. When managing a conflict caused by the gossip and criticism of a passive-aggressive employee, you should:
    A. Request a private meeting with the employee in which you directly confront the person about the gossip he has been spreading.
    B. Publicly confront the person about the gossip he has been spreading.
    C. Request a private meeting with the employee in which you first discuss his work responsibilities.

29. When you encounter an employee who tends to yell, "What the hell happened? Why aren't things ready? Another screwup!" you should respond by saying:
    A. "I understand you are upset. However, anger will not help. Let's discuss this matter more thoroughly in private."
    B. "If you have a better solution to the problem, I'd like to hear it."
    C. "This behavior is unacceptable. If you can't work with the team, we'll remove you from it."

Use the following scenario to answer questions 30–32:
As manager of a busy electronics store, you spot one of your employees, Alan, fixing a broken shelf in the back room while customers who need assistance are looking for help.

30. Say to your employee:
    A. "Alan, what are you doing back here?! Get out on the sales floor *now!*"
    B. "Alan, can you take care of that later? We've got a floor full of customers right now."
    C. "Alan, hurry up and fix that so you can get out on the sales floor to assist customers."

31. In order to help Alan better understand his job priorities, you should:
    A. Meet with Alan to discuss the questions, "What are you doing? How much time does it take? What gets in your way? And how much time do they take?"
    B. Conduct a private meeting with Alan, telling him that he gets paid to help customers, not perform maintenance activities.
    C. Hold a private meeting with Alan and ask him if he would prefer to take on a maintenance position.

32. To wrap up your meeting with Alan, you should:
    A. Tell Alan that if he doesn't want to do his job, he should find another place to work.
    B. Ask Alan to think about whether a different position at the company, such as maintenance, would suit him better.
    C. Review with Alan the activities on which he should focus his time.

Answer Key

Directions: Using the following key, compare your answers to the ones listed (see chart on the facing page). For every correct answer, give yourself 1 point in the Points column. For all wrong answers, give yourself 0 points in the Points column. Once you're finished scoring, total your points in the space marked Total.

Interpreting Your TIQ Assessment Results

Directions: Using your total score from the Answer Key, determine your overall Talent IQ.

Score	Talent IQ
30–32	**High Superior:** You demonstrate extensive knowledge and practical understanding of the course of action chosen by TalentLeaders.
26–29	**Superior:** You demonstrate significant knowledge and practical understanding of the course of action chosen by TalentLeaders.
20–25	**High Average:** You demonstrate basic knowledge and practical understanding of the course of action chosen by TalentLeaders.
9–19	**Average:** You demonstrate partial knowledge and practical understanding of the course of action chosen by TalentLeaders.
0–8	**Low Average:** You demonstrate cursory and intermittent knowledge and practical understanding of the course of action chosen by outstanding leaders.

Question # and Answer	Your Answer	Points
1. B		
2. A		
3. C		
4. B		
5. B		
6. A		
7. C		
8. C*		
9. A		
10. A		
11. C		
12. A		
13. A		
14. A		
15. B		
16. A		
17. A		
18. C		
19. B		
20. B		
21. A		
22. C		
23. B		
24. A		
25. C		
26. A		
27. C		
28. C		
29. A		
30. B		
31. A		
32. C		
		TOTAL:

*Though A and B can grow out of coaching, you should initially undertake C.

The TIQ Development Guide

Directions: Once you have obtained your overall TIQ score, you're ready to target specific areas for improvement. If you did not answer a question correctly, or if you answered it correctly but you're not sure why, consult the relevant chapter listed below. This can serve as your own personal improvement guide.

For Questions 1–4:
See Chapter 1, Build a Culture of Achievement

For Questions 5–7:
See Chapter 2, Select Achievers

For Questions 8–10:
See Chapter 3, Coach for Achievement

For Questions 11–13:
See Chapter 4, Improve or Remove Talent-on-the-Bubble

For Questions 14–19:
See Chapter 5, Communicate Commitment

For Questions 20–22:
See Chapter 6, Measure Responsibility

For Questions 23–25:
See Chapter 7, Improve Team IQ

For Questions 26–29:
See Chapter 8, Manage Conflict—Now!

For Questions 30–32:
See Chapter 9, Design a Leadership Talent Map for the Future

The Global Demographics of Talent

Hurricane Change

THE DEMOGRAPHICS OF talent have been changing at an astonishing rate. The United States, long the world leader in talent and innovation, now teeters on the brink of a talent shortage. In today's knowledge economy, which is driven by innovation and service, success hinges on the leadership abilities of knowledge workers, the individuals whose work revolves around information. Such work requires a new set of skills. Unfortunately, current trends show that the United States will struggle to compete with the rest of the world to create a competitive edge with these skills.

Four key factors are among those contributing to this predicament: education, the decline of men in the academic and professional worlds in the United States, outsourcing and offshoring, and an aging American work force.

Education

United States

Success in today's knowledge-based economy requires talented knowledge workers, but current trends indicate that the United

237

States is not educating enough of them. According to the *Busi-nessWeek* article "America the Uneducated," today 85 percent of American adults possess at least a high school diploma (up from 25 percent in 1940), and 28 percent have earned a college degree. While these numbers seem impressive, they do not tell the whole story. According to *BusinessWeek*, the number of high school and college graduates will not only grind to a standstill; it may actually decrease over the next fifteen years. If so, this puts the American economy at great risk.

In addition, those who are graduating from colleges and universities in the United States are not entering the fields so crucial to our economic success. The United States needs more people to fill high-tech jobs, such as engineering and IT, in order to compete in the new global economy. However, according to the *BusinessWeek* article "More Visas for High-Tech Workers May Be Inevitable," the U.S. Department of Education has reported that bachelor degrees awarded in electrical engineering declined 46 percent from 1987 to 1997. Obviously, this leaves the United States with a major shortage of critical talent.

Asia

While American students are losing ground academically, students in Asia are reaping the benefits of educational improvements in their countries. In the *U.S. News and World Report* article "Can America Keep Up?" David Calhoun, vice chairman of General Electric, issues this challenge to American students: "There are huge populations out there who are motivated beyond your imagination. That's what you're going to contend with. They didn't grow up with what you had, but they want it. And you can't believe how much studying goes on in those families." Unlike their American counterparts, Asian students hunger for success, and they will work tirelessly to achieve it. As Roy Singham, CEO of Thought-Works, says in the same article: "When you're in college drinking beer and watching the Super Bowl, your counterpart in China is on his fourth book."

More and more Asian countries particularly stress science and math, the two areas that drive cutting-edge new products and technological innovation. American eighth-graders rank ninth in science proficiency and fifteenth in math proficiency among forty-five countries, including Malaysia. In addition, according to "Can America Keep Up?" India, China, and South Korea now house many world-class schools, quite often affiliated with and under the guidance of top American institutions. This means fewer Asian students will attend school in the United States, where in the past they often remained to work.

According to the *BusinessWeek* article "Outsourcing Hasn't Hit Its Peak," government mandates and reforms also account for increased educational improvements in such countries as India. The literacy rate in India has risen from 20 percent in the 1980s to 70 percent today. In addition, according to the *McKinsey Quarterly* article "Ensuring India's Offshoring Future," India boasts 14 million university graduates, adding 2.5 million new ones every year, 1.5 times the number of China's graduates and almost twice that of the United States.

Europe

Every year, the European Union heads of government convene for the Lisbon agenda, a summit to discuss economic reform. According to the *Economist* article "Back to School," in 2006 the Lisbon agenda agreed that by 2010, the EU should strive to become the world's "most competitive and dynamic knowledge-based economy." However, Europe must implement major reforms in its school systems before it can possibly hope to achieve that goal.

According to "Back to School," Europe's problem starts at the secondary school level. A study run by the Organization for

239

Economic Cooperation and Development (OECD) rated the mathematics performance of an average fifteen-year-old from a big European country at or below the international average in a field where Hong Kong, South Korea, and Japan lead the pack.

When it comes to higher education, Europe also gets a failing grade. According to Shanghai's Jiao Tong University, currently seventeen of the top twenty universities in the world are American, and 32 percent of students who study outside of their home countries study in the United States. Although a recent report by the Organization for Economic Cooperation and Development (OECD) titled "Education at a Glance: OECD Indicators" shows that three European nations—Norway, Britain, and the Netherlands—have surpassed the United States in the proportion of young people who graduate from college, you can't take this at face value.

According to the *Chronicle of Higher Education* article "Falling Behind," the report indicates that from 1990 to 1997, the number of students enrolled in postsecondary education increased by more than 20 percent in all but five OECD-member countries, and by 50 percent in six OECD-member countries (Portugal, Poland, Hungary, Turkey, Britain, and the Czech Republic). However, these increases do not translate into large numbers of students because the countries operate such small college systems. For example, Portugal leads in enrollment growth, but only 7 percent of its population between the ages of twenty-five and sixty-four has attended college. In actual number of graduates, South Korea now surpasses Europe.

In terms of technical degrees, essential ingredients to any recipe to become the world's "most competitive and dynamic knowledge-based economy," the article "Back to School" reveals that China and India are producing more graduate engineers than the entire European Union. This puts Europe at a distinct disadvantage in today's knowledge-based economy.

Gender

United States

A startling new trend toward fewer and fewer men in the educational system also affects the talent pool. According to *College Enrollment and Work Activity of 2004 High School Graduates*, issued by the Bureau of Labor Statistics, of the 1.8 million youths attending college in October of 2004, young women accounted for 61.4 percent. In addition, the young women who enrolled in college were more likely than were the young men to graduate within six years. This trend, which does not appear to be slowing down, could have a major impact on America's economic and social structure. According to the AACRAO article "Colleges and Universities Attempt to Improve the Gender Gap," the severity of the gender gap has led many colleges and universities to consider affirmative action for men in order to achieve a greater gender balance. This means that if a male candidate and a female candidate possess equal qualifications, or, in some cases, even if the female possesses higher qualifications, a university will admit the male.

However, some universities have found other ways to attract men to their campuses. According to David Hawkins, director of public policy for the National Association for College Admission Counseling, "Now most four-year colleges work with their own internal marketing department or contract out to an independent agency that tailors their marketing plan to young men—and they are very, very aggressive."

Although the gender gap affects colleges and universities, it starts long before that.

A recent study by the U.S. Department of Education revealed that the gender gap in education starts as early as elementary school. According to the study, in elementary school, female fourth-graders outperformed their male peers in reading (2003) and writing (2002) assessments, and then have been getting closer in mathematics and science achievement. The gender differences

241

in the National Assessment of Educational Progress (NAEP) reading achievement grew from 10 points in 1999 to 16 points in 2002 at the secondary school level. These statistics speak to the need for more support for boys in the American educational system. U.S. Secretary of Education Rod Paige says, "It is clear that girls are taking education very seriously and that they have made tremendous strides. The issue now is that boys seem to be falling behind. We need to spend some time researching the problem so that we can give boys the support to succeed academically."

Ironically, although more women are graduating from college, they are underrepresented in many crucial fields of study, such as engineering, computer science, and the physical sciences. In fact, according to a survey of 385 colleges by the Higher Education Research Institute, University of California, Los Angeles, only 2.6 percent of this year's female college freshmen expect to major in engineering, compared to 15.6 percent of freshmen males. If more women majored in technical subjects, the United States would fare much better in competition with Asian countries.

Asia

According to the *BusinessWeek* article "America the Uneducated," while education declines in the United States, "education is exploding in countries such as China and India." (In India, the literacy rate in the 1980s was 20 percent; today it is 70 percent.) U.S. high school math and reading scores rank below those of most European and Asian economies, and now almost as many students attend college in China as in the United States. The Conference Board projects that within a decade, students in these countries will be as likely to get a high school education as will be their American counterparts, and due to their countries' populations, they will probably produce more college graduates. National Center for Public Policy and Higher Education president Patrick M. Callan warns that more U.S. white-collar jobs will move offshore. "For the U.S. economy, the implication of these trends is really stark."

In contrast to the United States, men continue to dominate both education and the work force in Asian countries such as China and India. Men outnumber women in secondary schools and higher education, a trend that will continue for many years to come, according to the *Reading Today* article "Bridging the Gender Gap." This underrepresentation of women in higher education and the work force stems largely from deep-seated cultural ideas about gender identity and the greater importance of education for boys.

In fact, according to the *Science* article "China Debates Big Drop in Women Physics Majors," an alarming trend is taking place in China: The number of women majoring in physics has sharply decreased. In the 1970s, more than one in three physics students at two of China's top universities were women, whereas today they make up fewer than one in ten. At Beijing University and Nanjing University, women accounted for an average of 42 percent and 37 percent of physics majors, respectively, but by the 1990s, those numbers plummeted to 9 percent and 8 percent.

This trend derives from the government's attitude toward technical workers. In the 1970s, when the government needed to produce large numbers of technical workers, it dictated what students should study. One Beijing University physics graduate, who originally planned to major in mathematics, recalls, "Many students who scored the highest marks in entrance examinations were assigned to study physics even if they did not apply for it." Thus, many women were forced into physics. Today, however, they are discouraged from doing so. Wu Ling'an, a senior physicist with the Chinese Academy of Sciences, observes: "It's better to choose a good husband and take care of the kids at home rather than working as a man's equal in the office or lab."

In order for women in Asian countries to enjoy the same educational and economic advantages as men, the existing societal views of women must change. This, however, will prove very difficult because, as Li Fanghua warns, "It's not so much discrimination as it is a legacy of feudal stereotypes."

Europe

The transition from industrial to knowledge economies has also created a gender gap in the European workplace.

According to the *U.S. News and World Report* article "Gender, Jobs and Economic Survival," in Britain, France, and Germany, "nonemployment" (the total number of registered unemployed workers plus those too discouraged to look for jobs) has tripled for men between the ages of twenty-five and fifty-five since 1970. From 1973 to 1992, male participation in the British work force decreased from 93 percent to 84 percent, with female participation rising from 53 percent to 65 percent. Seventy percent of the jobs created in Europe in the second half of the 1980s went to women and new entrants in the labor market, and by 1991, one-third of unskilled males were jobless in Britain. Furthermore, a study conducted by Warwick University's Institute of Employment Research projects that jobs performed by women in Britain will increase by 700,000, and those carried out by men will decrease by 200,000.

The increase in part-time jobs dramatically contributes to the gender gap. Two-thirds of all positions in OECD countries are service-sector jobs in areas such as health care, retail, travel, office, and telecommunications. Unfortunately, an increasing proportion of the work for these jobs requires only an average of fifteen hours of labor per week. In Britain, the number of full-time jobs recently decreased by 287,000, while the number of part-time jobs increased by 215,000. More women than men fill part-time positions, with women accounting for 85 percent of part-time workers in Britain.

These changes provide some disturbing short- and long-term implications. According to "Gender, Jobs and Economic Survival," part-time jobs allow employers to cut costs by reducing permanent payrolls, and women earn less per hour than the men in each of the

OECD nations. Due to the rise in female part-time employment, the average earning growth in Britain has dropped to thirty-year lows. And, as John Tomaney of Newcastle University's Center for Urban and Regional Development Studies warns: "We've created a huge male underclass in which crime and unemployment are a way of life. Our new economic base is very fragile."

Outsourcing and Offshoring

United States

With the American economy suffering a critical shortage of people trained in technology, more and more U.S. companies look elsewhere for that talent, outsourcing functions to such countries as China and India. Initially, companies outsourced to take advantage of what the *BusinessWeek* article "The Future of Outsourcing" calls "labor arbitrage," the wage gap between industrialized and developing nations. Now, however, companies often outsource to obtain *better talent* for less money.

This phenomenon completely alters the way the world does business. Given so many technology graduates in such countries as India and China, many companies now outsource their IT and other technology needs to them. The McKinsey Global Institute estimates that $18.4 billion in global IT work and $11.4 billion in business-process services has been shifted abroad so far, and this represents only one-tenth of the potential offshore market. But it goes far beyond IT work. According to Lakshmi Narayanan, chief executive of Cognizant Technology Solutions, many companies are outsourcing financial analysis to MBAs in India.

Two of the companies currently reaping the benefits of these services are GE and McKinsey. According to the *BusinessWeek* article "Outsourcing: Spreading the Gospel," McKinsey realized that it could create a world of "remote services" in which providers as far away as India and China could work for customers in the United States. In 1995, the company established the Knowledge Center in Delhi, where researchers would crunch numbers, analyze trends, and create PowerPoint presentations for McKinsey consultants worldwide. In 1996, when GE Capital experienced a shortage of talent needed to sustain the growth of its mortgage refinance business, the firm set up a small support office in Delhi. Once consultants and executives from these two organizations saw the benefits of outsourcing, they began leaving to start their own businesses, using offshore talent.

According to "The Future of Outsourcing," "it is becoming possible to buy, off the shelf, practically any function you need to run a company." For example, if you want to start an airline but you don't want to invest in a huge back office, a company called Navitaire will handle reservations, plan routes, assign crew, and calculate prices for each seat. Or, if you have developed a new product but you don't employ any market researchers, you can hire Evalueserve Inc., a New Delhi–based analytics outfit, to assemble a team of Indian patent attorneys, engineers, and business analysts who will mine global databases and call dozens of U.S. experts and wholesalers to provide an independent appraisal, all for just $5,000 a day.

However, despite the fear that the United States will lose jobs to offshoring, many experts now believe that the United States can benefit from the development. As stated in "The Future of Outsourcing," many executives now favor "transformational outsourcing," a more strategic view of global sourcing. Here, executives tap offshoring to fuel corporate growth, making better use of skilled staff in the United States and creating jobs here. Many companies now offshore work in order to free up their analysts, engineers, and salespeople from routine tasks, liberating them to focus their talent on innovating and dealing with customers. This approach to offshoring relies less on saving money than on growing the organization.

While the effects of offshoring on the United States's economy remain to be seen, one thing seems certain: This trend does not show any sign of slowing down; in fact, it has been gaining momentum.

Asia

No region has benefited more from outsourcing and offshoring than Asia, particularly India. American businesses seeking talented technical specialists have looked abroad to such Asian countries as China and India, both of which produce more technical workers than other countries. Not only that, but these workers bring strong credentials and a stronger work ethic to their jobs than do many American technical workers.

According to the *McKinsey Quarterly* article "Ensuring India's Offshoring Future," India ranks as the world's largest and fastest-growing offshoring sector. In low-level jobs? No, in IT services, which play a major role in the country's overall economic growth. According to the article, in 2004–2005, India's offshore IT and business-process outsourcing industry generated approximately $17.3 billion in revenue and employed around 695,000 people. By 2007–2008 that work force may include 1,450,000 to 1,550,000 people, accounting for 7 percent of India's GDP.

Although India's dominance of offshoring will not wane soon, some analysts think that India's talent pool may be shrinking. According to "Ensuring India's Offshoring Future," when rated for their suitability for employment by multinational companies, a significant number of India's huge supply of graduates fail to make the grade because they lack significant English language skills. Due to customer complaints about communication with Indian operators, many U.S. companies have shifted their call centers from India to the Philippines.

Additionally, only 1.2 million Indians (4 percent of the total university-educated work force) hold engineering degrees, compared with 33 percent in China. India may well experience a shortage of engineers within the next few years. However, India does offer a large talent pool for non-IT services, such as R & D, finance and accounting, call centers, and back-office administration.

Europe

In order to remain competitive on a global scale, European countries have also rushed into outsourcing and offshoring. According to the *VNUNET* article "Europe Outsourcing Capital of the World," Europe has now overtaken the United States as the world's leading market for outsourcing contracts. The dramatic rise in offshoring in Europe has come about because Europe must keep up with other multinationals that earlier took the outsourcing path.

In the *BusinessWeek* article "Job Exports: Europe's Turn," Chris Gentle, European research director for Deloitte, says, "If you're competing against someone like Citigroup, which has grown revenues three times faster than costs [through extensive outsourcing to India], you really don't have a choice. It's changing the operating model of European institutions." Thus, Deloitte Research estimates that about 800,000 financial-services and high-tech jobs will migrate from Western Europe to cheaper labor markets, principally India, but also Eastern Europe and China.

According to the *BusinessWeek* article "Offshoring: The Pros and Cons for Europe," offshoring can enable European countries to slash service costs by 50–60 percent. And many companies can offshore half or more of their sales, general, and administrative expenses. With offshoring, many European companies can raise profits and reduce prices and become more competitive, which will help keep inflation in check.

Although many people in the United States fear losing jobs to outsourcing and offshoring, Europeans face even graver consequences. According to "Offshoring: The Pros and Cons for Europe," two critical components determine a nation's offshoring benefits: redeployment (or what percentage of workers who lose jobs can find new ones), and recapture (or what percentage of the wages paid in lost jobs are recaptured by the wages paid in new ones). Unfortunately, with the exception of Britain, whose flexible economy could quickly create new jobs, Europe's rigid employment practices and labor rules mean very few new jobs created for displaced workers. Because of this, the overall unemployment rate may increase, with a consequent reduction of overall income.

Aging Work Force

United States

Gone are the days when companies offered early-retirement packages to older employees so they could make way for newer, younger workers, largely because the United States will soon face a serious labor shortage. The baby-boom generation, the 76 million Americans born between 1946 and 1964, is poised to retire within the next ten years. According to the *BusinessWeek* article "Keep Boomers on the Job," that's a full 43 percent of the U.S. work force. This many people retiring over such a short time span will adversely affect the American work force as it loses the talent, skills, and practical judgment this generation has gained from a lifetime of working.

Adding to the problem, the next two generations of workers are each 15 percent smaller than the baby-boom generation. According to the Microsoft article "Shifting Workplace Demographics and Delayed Retirement," the portion of the work force aged twenty-five to thirty-nine will decline 5.7 percent by 2010. Also, according to the Employment Policy Foundation, the work force will experience a shortfall of 7.4 million baccalaureate degree holders by 2012.

The good news: due to increased life expectancy (up from forty-seven years in 1900 to seventy-seven years today), more people are delaying retirement. A Merrill Lynch retirement survey of 3,000 baby boomers found that 83 percent intend to remain in the work

249

force. The article "Shifting Workplace Demographics and Delayed Retirement" claims that by 2010, more than 51 percent of the work force will be forty or older. These people either need the income or wish to remain professionally active, maintain mental alertness, and keep engaged in their communities. Some opt to keep or modify their existing jobs, some choose to work full- or part-time at new jobs, and some elect to become mentors to younger workers. More people remaining in the work force will alleviate the effects of a talent shortage in the United States. In addition, the younger generation of workers will reap the benefits of the skills, knowledge, and values of more experienced workers.

Asia

Like the United States, Asia will soon feel the effects of a rapidly aging population. Countries there will also be facing the fact that while so many of their workers are aging and retiring, fewer young workers will come along to take their place, creating a critical shortage of talent.

According to a report by IBM Business Consulting Services titled "Challenges of an Aging Workforce," Japan may fall victim to the most severe demographic crisis in Asia. Within the next ten years, more than 33 million people (26 percent of the population) will be over sixty-five years old. Due to the low birthrate in Japan (1.3 children for each woman), by 2050 Japan's population will drop from 127 million to about 100 million, eliminating a third of the country's labor force.

According to the report, China's situation may not be as grave as Japan's, but it too will suffer the effects of an aging talent pool. Today, only 11 percent of the population is over sixty, but the United Nations projects that by 2040 it will increase by 28 percent. This means 397 million people over sixty-five, which exceeds the current populations of France, Germany, Italy, Japan, and the United Kingdom combined. Because of the transformation from state-run enterprises with generous benefits to private corporations with few, if any, retirement benefits, hundreds of millions of workers may not fare well in their retirement years.

However, as with the United States, Asian nations can benefit from their aging work force: attracting and retaining older workers on a part-time or flex-time basis, mentoring, and updating aging workers' skills.

Europe

While many economies around the globe will feel the effects of an aging work force, none will feel it more than Europe. Just as in the United States and Asia, Europe is experiencing an increase in life expectancy and a decrease in birthrates. However, Europe's disparity makes theirs pale by comparison.

According to the *Washington Post* article "'Old Europe' and Getting Older," a person born today in Germany, France, or Italy will live to seventy-eight years, compared to sixty-seven years in the 1950s. Additionally, the number of births per woman has decreased dramatically: in France, 1.7; in Germany, 1.4; in Italy, 1.2; and in Spain, 1.16, the lowest recorded in human history. According to "Addressing the Challenges of an Aging Workforce," over the next two decades the number of people aged fifty to sixty-four will increase by 25 percent, whereas those aged twenty to twenty-nine will decrease by 20 percent, meaning not enough people will enter the work force to replace the older workers.

Generous state pensions offered by many European countries exacerbate the problem. For example, according to the *Business-Week* article "Global Aging," Jenny Francois has worked in data entry for insurer Macif in Agen, France, for twenty years. For the past three years, she has been in "pre-retirement," working just two days a week and still collecting $1,500 a month (more than 70 percent of her previous full-time salary). When she reaches sixty, her pay will decline only slightly. However, with the combination of an aging population and a low birthrate, workers like Francoise will not be able to enjoy such lavish benefits much longer. Because many economists fear that this combination will lead to bankrupt pensions and lower living standards by midcentury, many countries have begun cutting back on once-lucrative retirement benefits.

Europe's aging work force will lead to a talent shortage. According to the IBM report "Addressing the Challenges of an Aging Workforce," in a 2002 study of more than 500 German companies, 23 percent stated that the aging population represented a problem for their organizations, and 39 percent indicated they were facing challenges due to shortages of qualified labor. The loss of older workers from the European work force means a loss of expertise when knowledge does not pass on to the next generation of workers. This loss of expertise includes insights on managing key customer relationships and handling exceptions to critical processes, which cost organizations time, energy, and resources to replace.

In order to alleviate the situation, Europe, like the United States and Asia, has begun to implement many new strategies to keep people in the work force longer, including an increased retirement age, and stricter criteria for workers earning pensions. Many individual companies hope to retain current older workers and attract new older workers by allowing them to work part-time or flexible schedules, and giving them the opportunity to update their skills. They are also taking the time to preserve the knowledge of older workers before they leave the company so that their knowledge can be passed on to other generations of workers. These initiatives, and others, will help Europe keep its economy afloat in the wake of its changing population.

Conclusion

In order to succeed in today's economy, the United States must actively address the talent shortage crisis. Steps should include reforming our educational system, which produces so much of our country's talent. Without more educated men in our work force, and without more emphasis on technology, the United States will fall behind in the new knowledge economy. The United States must also find ways to utilize the skills and talents of its aging workers or risk losing one of its most valuable assets.

Bibliography: The Global Demographics of Talent

"Back to School." *The Economist*, 25 Mar. 2006, 58.

"Bridging the Gender Gap." *Reading Today* 21 (2003/2004): 1–5.

"College Enrollment and Work Activity of 2004 High School Graduates." U.S. Department of Labor: Bureau of Labor Statistics. *www.bls.gov/news.release/hsgec.nr0.htm.*

"The McKinsey Global Survey of Business Executives, March 2004." *The McKinsey Quarterly*, 2006. McKinsey & Company. 28 Feb. 2006. *www.mckinseyquarterly.com.*

"Outsourcing Hasn't Hit Its Peak." *BusinessWeek*, 17 Feb. 2006. *BusinessWeek Online: www.businessweek.com.*

"Shifting Workplace Demographics and Delayed Retirement." Microsoft 9, Oct. 2005. 1 Mar. 2006. *www.microsoft.com/enable/aging/demographics.aspx?v=t.*

"Study Shows Educational Achievement Gender Gap Shrinking." U.S. Department of Education, 2 Mar. 2006. *www.ed.gov/news/pressreleases/2004/11/11192004b.html.*

Craig, David, and Paul Willmott. "Outsourcing Grows Up." *The McKinsey Quarterly.* 2006. McKinsey & Company. *www.mckinseyquarterly.com.*

Engardio, Pete, Arndt, Michael, and Dean Foust. "The Future of Outsourcing." *BusinessWeek*, 30 Jan. 2006. *BusinessWeek Online*: *www.businessweek.com/magazine/content/06_05/b3969401.htm*.

Engardio, Pete, et al. "Global Aging." *BusinessWeek*, 31 Jan. 2005. *BusinessWeekOnline*: *www.businessweek.com/Print/magazine/content/05_05/b3918011.htm?chan=gl*.

Farrell, Chris. "The Global Spread of Higher Ed." *BusinessWeek*, 28 Nov. 2005. *BusinessWeek Online*, 28 Feb. 2006. *www.business week.com*.

Farrell, Diana, Noshir Kaka, and Sascha Sturze. "Ensuring India's Offshoring Future." *The McKinsey Quarterly*, 2006. McKinsey & Company. *www.mckinseyquarterly.com*.

Garten, Jeffrey E. "Keep Boomers on the Job." *BusinessWeek*, 14 Nov. 2005. *BusinessWeek Online*: *www.businessweek.com/print/magazine/content/05_46/b3959159.htm?chan=gl*.

Ghosh, Palash. "A Word to the Wise Investor: Demographics." *BusinessWeek*, 4 Aug. 2005. *BusinessWeek Online*: *www.business week.com*.

Gutner, Toddi. "When You Still Want to Work." *BusinessWeek*, 25 July 2005. *BusinessWeek Online*: *www.businessweek.com/print/magazine/content/05_30/b3944420.htm?chan=gl*.

Hof, Robert. "Silicon Valley's Call: Smarten Up, America!" *BusinessWeek*, 17 Nov. 2005. *BusinessWeek Online*: *www.businessweek.com*.

Jacques, Robert. "Europe Outsourcing Capital of the World." *VNUNET*, 14 Jan. 2005. *www.vnunet.com/vnunet/news/2126512/europe-outsourcing-capital-world*.

254

Jianxiang, Yang. "China Debates Big Drop in Women Physics Majors." *Science* 11 (Jan. 2002): 263.

Knight, Robin. "Gender, Jobs and Economic Survival." *U.S. News and World Report*, 19 Sept. 1994, 63.

Kripalani, Manjeet, and Brian Grow. "Offshoring: Spreading the Gospel." *BusinessWeek*, 6 Mar. 2006. *BusinessWeek Online: www .businessweek.com*.

Lesser, Eric, Bill Farrell, and Meredith Payne. "Addressing the Challenges of an Aging Workforce: A Human Capital Perspective for Firms Operating in Asia Pacific." IBM Corporation, 21 Oct. 2004. IBM Corporation: *www-1.ibm.com/services/us/index.wss/ibvstudy/ imc/a1005502?cntxt=a1005263*.

Lesser, Eric, Carsten Hausmann, and Steffen Feuerpeil. "Addressing the Challenges of an Aging Workforce: A Human Capital Perspective for Companies Operating in Europe." IBM Corporation, 16 Mar. 2005. IBM Corporation: *www-1.ibm.com/services/us/index .wss/ibvstudy/bcs/a1009193?cntxt=a1000407*.

Mandel, Michael, Steve Hamm, and Christopher J. Farrell. "Why the Economy Is a Lot Stronger Than You Think." *BusinessWeek*, 13 Feb. 2006. *BusinessWeek Online: www.businessweek.com/magazine/ toc/06_07/B3971magazine.htm*.

Matlack, Carol, et al. "Job Exports: Europe's Turn." *BusinessWeek*, 19 April 2004. *BusinessWeek Online: www.businessweek.com*.

Newman, Richard J. "Can America Keep Up?" *U.S. News and World Report*, 27 Mar. 2006. *www.usnews.com/usnews/biztech/articles/ 060327/27global.htm*.

Shipman, William G. "'Old Europe' and Getting Older." *The Washington Post*, 14 May 2003. CATO Institute, *www.cato.org/research/articles/shipman-030514.html*.

Sostek, Anya. "Who Gets In? Gender Can Be Blessing or Curse in College Admission." *Pittsburgh Post-Gazette*, 15 Feb. 2006. *www.post-gazette.com/pg/pp/06046/655194.stm*.

Straight, Susan. "More Visas for High-Tech Workers May Be Inevitable." *BusinessWeek*, 23 Mar. 2000. *BusinessWeek Online: www.businessweek.com*.

Symonds, William C. "America the Uneducated." *BusinessWeek*, 21 Nov. 2005. *BusinessWeek Online: www.businessweek.com/print/magazine/content/05_47/b3960108.htm?chan=gl*.

Tyson, Laura D'Andrea. "Offshoring: The Pros and Cons for Europe." *BusinessWeek*, 6 Dec. 2004. *BusinessWeek Online: www.businessweek.com*.

Wheeler, David. "Falling Behind." *Chronicle of Higher Education*, 26 May 2000: A63.

Wolf, Rachel. "Women Need Math-Esteem and Larger Numbers in Jobs." *The Mercury News*, 28 Feb. 2006. *www.mercurynews.com/mld/mercurynews/living/people/teens/13980066.htm*.

Zimar, Heather. "Colleges and Universities Attempt to Improve the Gender Gap." AACRAO 2001. American Association of Collegiate Registrars and Admissions Officers. 3 Mar. 2006. *www.aacrao.org/transcript/index.cfm?fuseaction=show_print&doc_id=3061*.

The Talent IQ Research Project

WE INVITE READERS to contact us for additional information and for excerpts from the EC Murphy Walsh corporate study, *Talent IQ: A Comprehensive Study of Talent Management Practices in the Global Economy.*

The study involved leaders from EC Murphy Walsh client organizations (543) and non-client organizations (2,200), whom we invited to participate in the Talent IQ research project. Of the total, 411 and 572, respectively, participated, providing a representative sample of 983 organizations from the arenas of business, health care, charitable and not-for-profit public service, and government.

We asked leaders to identify talented individuals in their organizations who might participate in the study (those making significant contributions to their organizations at a level of 6 or 7 on a 7 point performance scale). Over a ten-year period we studied a grand total of 102,317 individuals.

To facilitate the use of survey instruments and multivariate analyses, we extracted samples for various specific purposes (as cited in the book and in the research monograph). These included samples of average and low-performing subjects in various categories, including managers, team leaders, professionals, and frontline workers in an assortment of occupational classifications. We also drew upon the samples for focus group testing and discussion, as well as for individual interviewing.

The process included both proprietary EC Murphy Walsh surveys and analyses and a number of other established psychological assessments used to compare and validate similarities and differences as suggested by specific research needs. The results confirmed the validity and reliability of the achievement trait profile and other results presented in the book at a .01 confidence level or better. An annotated bibliography regarding research by others on the seven characteristics of achievement is presented in a corporate white paper and is available upon request. Research on individual characteristics provides insight into how the characteristics were likely adopted by TalentLeaders in the process of their personal and professional life experiences.

All other results, case studies, conceptual models, and tools were either developed during the Talent IQ research process to address specific needs arising from the data or to probe for more insight into best practices.

Please contact us at *ECMurphy@ecmurphywalsh.com.*

Index

Achievement. *See also* Building
 culture of achievement;
 Coaching for achievement;
 Selecting achievers
 defined, 5
 innovation and, 24, 25, 36
 leveraging power of, 22–23
 management and, 24, 25, 36
 perfect model of, 23–25
 pluralism and, 33
 principles of, summary, xiv, 4
 service and, 23–25, 35–36
 three paths of, developing,
  23–25
Achievement in Action Grid, xv,
 35–36, 37, 44, 89, 92–93, 99
Affiliative/power-driven
 organizations, 2, 3, 7, 25, 30–31,
 75, 164
Ambition
 becoming arrogance, x
 commitment and, 16
 George Armstrong Custer failure
  and, ix–x
 hiring, 183
Analytical approach
 to communication, 111, 112,
  113, 114, 115
 to problem-solving, 58, 60–61,
  65–66, 68, 69, 152, 153, 188
Apathy, 34
Aristocrats, 87–88, 122–23
Attenuation, 107–8, 109

Backstabber path, 75–76, 78
Ben & Jerry's, 9–10

Berry, Dr. Franklin, 31
Bomber behavior, 77, 82, 179–80,
 181–82
Bruggemann, Warren, 91–92, 186,
 204
Building culture of achievement,
 xiv, 1–25
 accepting responsibility and,
  19–21
 affiliative/power-driven
  organizations vs., 2, 3, 7, 25,
  30–31, 75, 164
 Ben & Jerry's example, 9–10
 benefits of, 2
 commitment to, 15–16
 embracing achievement, 5–7
 FDR assistant (Livingston
  Houston) example, 17–19
 formula overview, xiv, 3
 Intel (Andy Grove) example,
  5–7
 leveraging power of
  achievement, 22–23
 Malden Mills (Aaron Feuerstein)
  case study, 20–21
 optimism and, 17–19
 partnering with customers and,
  11–15, 16
 pragmatism and, 7–8
 reasons for, 2
 strategic humility and, 8–11, 17,
  46, 88
 talent curve and, 22
 Thomas Edison example, 7–8
 three paths of achievement and,
  23–25

About the Author

Emmett C. Murphy is chairman of EC Murphy Walsh, LLC, an international consulting firm specializing in the fields of talent leadership selection and development. He is the founder and former chairman and CEO of E.C. Murphy VHA, LLC, the world's largest business and healthcare alliance specializing in business restructuring and executive development. He has served as faculty and consultant for Brigham and Women's Hospital/Harvard School of Medicine, MIT's Sloan School of Management, Booz Allen Hamilton, and London University. He serves clients in business, government, and public service including IBM, Chase Manhattan, Hewlett-Packard, and the Department of Defense.

Murphy is the author of the *New York Times* business bestseller *Leadership IQ*; his other books include *Leading on the Edge of Chaos*; *The Genius of Sitting Bull: 13 Heroic Strategies for Business Leaders*; and *The New Murphy's Law*. His books and research have been featured in *USA Today* and the *New York Times*, and he has appeared on ABC, CBS, CNN, and NPR. He holds a PhD in organizational psychology from the State University of New York, with postdoctoral studies in organizational development and clinical counseling. He and his wife, Carol, reside in upstate New York. He can be contacted by e-mail at *ECMurphy@ECMurphyWalsh.com*.